Lost Wax

CRUX

THE GEORGIA SERIES IN LITERARY NONFICTION

John Griswold, *series editor*

LOST WAX

Essays / Jericho Parms

THE UNIVERSITY OF GEORGIA PRESS

ATHENS

© 2016 by the University of Georgia Press
Athens, Georgia 30602
www.ugapress.org
All rights reserved
Designed by Erin Kirk New
Set in 9/13 Joanna Nova

Most University of Georgia Press titles are
available from popular e-book vendors.

Printed digitally

Library of Congress Cataloging-in-Publication Data

Names: Parms, Jericho.
Title: Lost wax : essays / Jericho Parms.
Description: Athens : The University of Georgia Press, 2016. |
Series: Crux: the Georgia series in literary nonfiction ; 4 |
Includes bibliographical references.
Identifiers: LCCN 2016014288 (print) | LCCN 2016028277 (ebook) |
ISBN 9780820350158 (pbk. : alk. paper) | ISBN 9780820350141 (Ebook)
Classification: LCC PS3616.A759 A6 2016 (print) | LCC PS3616.A759 (ebook) |
DDC 814/.6—dc23
LC record available at https://lccn.loc.gov/2016014288

For my
mother—
and for poetry.

The young.
Maybe they'll let us be in their dreams.
—MATTHEW ZAPRUDER

CONTENTS

I

Girl Looking at the Sole of Her Foot

On Touching Ground

Deep within the galleries of the Metropolitan, a glass wall case barely contains the wild form of a racehorse. Veiny grooves mark the horse's flank and haunches, its powerful shoulders, crest, the forelock of its mane. The tail extends like a petticoat train in its cantering wake. Head high, the horse is poised, proud.

Perhaps even more than his dancers, more than his nude women bathing, horses captured the heart of Edgar Degas. Yet they all shared similar traits—in their ephemeral postures, in their show jumps and pliés, in the strength and energy of their legs cast in bronze. I peer in close. All four of the horse's hooves are suspended in midair.

Degas's bronze is polished, near black. The light catches the horse's muscular limbs, like white wax on obsidian, the patent leather shoes I wore as a girl in the city, or the riding boots I packed when we traveled west to Grandfather's ranch. Christmas in Arizona rarely brought snow. The desert floor left a coat of dust on my rubber soles.

In the mornings I helped Grandfather in the tack shed. The straw-scented air from the paddock mingled with the damp, industrial interior that sheltered old oil drums, mud-caked basins, ropes, harnesses, thrush ointments, and salve. I followed as he worked, measuring feed buckets, dragging water to the trough, grooming the remaining mares as their black marble eyes and mahogany bay coats shimmered in the sun.

———

I read in the newspapers that the wild mustangs are on the run again. Nearly thirty thousand horses still roam the open range. Each fall the papers grapple to tell the story of the annual rundown and removal of horses from public grazing lands. Decades since Congress passed the Wild Horse and Burro Act in 1971, prohibiting the capture of wild horses by machine for commercial sale, the *New York Times* described the latest roundup as "horse versus helicopter here in the high desert." Each year the occasion stirs controversy and I find myself, a world away, awaiting the whinny and squeal of the Manhattan-bound #1 train on my way to work at the museum, enmeshed in following the debate. For every advocate that warns of the damage—foals separated from their mothers, yearlings caught in the stampede—a straight-talking rancher heralds the old days of feral pursuit, when "a cowboy really wasn't a cowboy if you didn't rope a wild horse." The horses no longer vie against lasso-wielding cowboys and Indians; the Bureau of Land Management and its band of modern ranchers run down the horses with low-flying helicopters into makeshift corrals. Degas may have captured his racehorse in trot, but what of a wild-blooded mustang on the run?

Bronze bears no witness to a horse's speed. Whether by breeding or birthright, a horse is a runner, surrendering only to the curl and surge of its legs, to its hooves drumming the ground like thunder, to its mane fanning as it leans into each turn. I imagine the uneven terrain as a mere notion beneath their hooves, the same way the cracks in the concrete had no impact on me as I skipped down city streets; of no consequence were the tar pebbles and schist that got caught in my worn tennis shoes when I ran.

———

Out west, we sprinted like thoroughbreds. *Equus caballus.* Born of the same pedigree, my older brother and I were three years apart and an uneven match as we raced the dirt roads of my grandfather's Tucson ranch. I trailed, breathless. The warmth rose in my legs; my pulse quickened. My feet propelled me down the straight toward Grandfather's angled figure, his blue jeans pale with the dust of my brother's victory. But there he was, still palming his Stetson, its buckle gleaming as he swept his arm, waving me to the finish. A deep "whoa, whoa" sounded from his chest as I came to a stop in his arms. Leaning against his hip, my legs tingled—a slow sequence toward stillness—with each recaptured breath.

———

In 1878, Eadwaerd Muybridge—pioneer of the moving image—shot a series of photographs at the racetracks in Palo Alto, California. The images, *Horse in Motion*, revealed for the first time that there is a moment during a horse's trot when all four hooves simultaneously leave the ground. The previously unobserved phenomenon caused a sensation.

Muybridge toured Europe with his signature biunial lantern slides to present his sequence, which proved that artists, by depicting at least one hoof on the ground, had been misrepresenting the true movement of horses for ages.

Degas's horse is true to life. The artist frequented the Longchamp Racecourse in Paris to observe the racing breeds. He studied Muybridge's photographs and, by placing a supporting post beneath the horse's abdomen, molded each leg faithfully aloft. *Horse Trotting, Feet Not Touching Ground* is sleek, agile. But it is not on the run. Notice the upright neck and slightly gapped muzzle. Notice the stately curve from the crest to the loins and hindquarters, between the shoulders and breast—ribs open, posture squared, well trained, *rehearsed*. Degas has mastered a refined, elegant trot.

—————

In the museum, a girl enters the gallery where I linger after a lunch break. She scans the collection in a nearby wall case—*Horse Balking, Horse Rearing, Horse at Trough*—and then turns suddenly and increases her clip toward the adjacent gallery where a bronze dancer stands poised. Tiptoeing around the base, the girl peers up at the statuette fashioned with a corset and crinoline skirt. The statue's braided hair, cast in wax from a horsehair wig, is held by a bow of white satin. The dancer's legs support the upright carriage of her stance—fourth position, is it?—her right leg extending forward to present the inner line of her slippered foot while her left remains grounded. From behind, one can see her arms are locked close along the curve of her torso; her hands are cupped *a derrière*.

The Little Fourteen-Year-Old Dancer is modeled after the young ballerina Marie van Goethem, who became Degas's signature model and muse for his scrutiny of the female form in motion. Her figure, and those of several smaller dancers exhibited nearby, reveals the nuances of youth with subtle majesty—the soft tension between a prepubescent slouch and a choreographed style. Notice the *Dancer Putting On Her Stocking*, or another, *Looking at the Sole of Her Right Foot*, their nascent curiosity and preoccupation, the truth of their form—over their loveliness—revealing grace. From a distance, I can see that the bronze of the dancer's skin is tinted lighter than the trotting horse before me, more brown than black, like an equine coat of chestnut or roan, like the Sonoran sands after a heavy rain.

—————

At dusk, my grandfather and I walked away from the white adobe ranch house, along the back acres of his land. I skipped alongside him, keeping pace in the lines of his Bill Hickok shadow, which lay like a paper doll against the ground. And I, his devoted Calamity Jane. After a while, he stopped to square his legs and shoulders, as I grabbed his arms and stepped onto his boot tops. There, we waltzed. His white hair feathered around his head; his Buddy Holly glasses slid down his nose as he laughed. He smelled of pipe tobacco, hay bales, leather, and liniment—far from the cufflinks and fresh-laundered lapels he might have worn to white-tie affairs after he married my grandmother and settled back east. We danced until dark, his spurs scrawling arabesques in the dust, my feet safely elevated atop his. I could have been Marie van Goethem herself. The young dancer's head tilts upward. In the museum, as I stand before her, my own neck cranes. The statuette's eyes appear half-closed, as if wishing, or remembering, or searching to find her pose—like a rider feeling for balance on a saddle or a child seeking treasures of the past.

———

It's funny really, all this talk of horses. I was hardly the vision of a girl one might imagine on a horse: blue eyes and tight ponytail, beige riders and good posture. Nor was I the plaid-shirted cowgirl type with authentic chaps and true-buckle riding boots. With my blonde nappy curls and hand-me-downs, I may have been more akin to a horse than a rider. Born of a black father and white mother whose marriage in 1976 (nearly a decade after Loving v. Virginia struck down laws opposing interracial marriage) never really garnered approval from the families, each camp fearing how hard it might be for the children.

———

Before dark, my brother and I marked "X" in the grainy desert soils. Kneeling in the rocky arroyo, we staked our claim in the prospect of fool's gold and muscovite to add to the growing museum of specimens we brought back to the city: flint arrowheads and fossil shells, horse-shoes and snake skins, a handful of sharks' teeth buffed and blackened from the Gulf Coast of Mexico. We collected what we could. Back home, we became the curators, turning the windowsills of our bedroom into showcases, testimonies of a land otherwise odd and foreign to us "city kids." And what we couldn't bring back I recorded in the archives of memory: Grandfather's dalmatian prancing among the horses; a gestating mare bedding down in straw; the first steps of a newborn foal, gray-moistened with life, eager to unfold its legs, to stand, wobble, run. This became our gallery, evidence of the expanse of life and what it meant to dream.

———

Degas had his evidence. He learned about movement from the sequential photographs of Muybridge, the world-class racing breeds at Longchamp, and van Goethem and her classmates at L'École de Danse of the Paris Opera. Degas molded his horses with the same painstaking observation as he did his female figures: a galloping stride captured with equal scrutiny as a woman's step from a bath or a ballerina's pointe work. In the same way Muybridge revealed the nature of human and animal locomotion—a *Horse and Rider Galloping*, a *Woman Opening a Parasol*, *Man and Woman Dancing a Waltz*—Degas revealed the common repertoire of movement, of finesse.

Perhaps that is why children seem to appreciate the Degas galleries. They filter in and out with wide eyes, parents somewhere in tow, or enter with the brisk run-walk of field trip excitement. They peer at the pastel canvases of dancers stretching at the barre, or the bronze statuettes midpirouette. The girls finger-brush their hair and retie their ponytails, mimicking the footwork. One girl demonstrates a *pas-de-bourrée* shift to *demi-plié*. The museum's wood floor creaks beneath her. Another presses close against the wall case to better see the horses. She shimmies her shoulders, and I hear a faint "neigh" escape her pouty lips. I wonder what she sees, what world inhabits Degas's racehorse, what fate awaits her memories. Her fingers and nose leave breathy smudges that slowly vanish from the glass.

Much of what we know is emblematic: the glory of the West, the icon of a wild horse. Most of what we see is representation: the aesthetic of a captured pose, the inner compositions of how and why we remember. But some things we know because they are part of us: the long limbs and piano fingers I inherited from my grandfather, his high-arched feet and his curiosity, too. And some things we only know by observing: sequential images, dominant traits, language used to classify, shape, and mold.

For my grandfather's part, it was a simple choice to live in the Sonora—to "go west" as he did—from the valleys of Pennsylvania to the Arizona plains where, in the late 1930s, he worked his way through college. And there, by chance, he met my grandmother, the fair-skinned, blonde-bobbed young woman on an English saddle, who was traveling on a sorority vacation. Grandfather rescued her from a runaway horse. I've imagined the story more than once: a harem of Bettys and Dorothys touring the desert on horseback, when one takes off from the caravan. Did my grandmother will her horse to gallop, or did it take off beneath her? Did Grandfather feel his horse's hooves aloft as he followed in pursuit? The two of them later settled back east, but they always plotted to retire, as they did in the mid-1970s, on the same land where they first surveyed their courtship.

I, too, moved west for college, and then for a while I just kept going: West to Southwest, Central America, and eventually Europe, moving between the backcountry and the boroughs, and always returning to New York. I sometimes wonder to what extent I was still running in search of the thrill I felt twirling atop my grandfather's boots or racing toward a mirage.

We never know how much we inherit from the past. How far did the early stagecoaches travel to stake claims on new land? How far did Degas voyage through the Parisian racetracks and ballet theaters to capture his forms? How far ahead did my grandfather plan to escape the domestic landscape of the suburbs and cities, to return to his unfettered freedom?

———

Few sights compare to that of a wild mustang. *Equus ferus*. First introduced to the Americas by Spanish conquistadors, many of the feral horse breeds left free on the range descended from cavalry horses once bred for their size and strength. Grandfather, docent of my curiosity, taught me of the wild horses—*los mesteños*, the stray, the "ownerless"—of what they teach us about resilience and grace. For those he owned on the ranch—retired quarter horses and show breeds—we rehearsed every act of their care: testing the water temperature, tasting the feed. We sampled the liniment, too, used to cool the horses in the Tucson heat. I watched him as he rubbed it into his own skin. "Whatever is good enough for the horses" was good enough for him. So I tried it too, massaging a dab on my knees and ankles, kneading the thin muscles along my shins. The balm tingled and burned. My skin felt like ice (not just cold, but colorless), polished, sleek. I almost believed that we could feel what the horses felt, that our legs could know what their legs knew:

about the difference between a trot and a run, between mere movement and dancing—that freedom is different from flight.

And maybe we are among those untamed and unclassified, neither domestic nor wild—half-breeds given just enough training in the world to watch our backs in the city before we are let free to live and graze with abandon, forming our own names for things that exist between extremes (neither the saddle nor the shoe, wax nor the obsidian).

Sometimes I think that as long as the horses are left free to roam, memory, too, may exist unbound. Yet each fall bands of mustangs are corralled into holding pens. Of those that survive the stampedes, some will be trapped and tamed, preserved as keepsakes or insignia, like the cast of an infant's shoe enclosed in a museum vitrine. Some will be broken and trained like a ballerina forced to shed her youth. But some will run like the racehorses of Longchamp, like a runaway stallion courting romance, and escape to another year, trotting, until the day their feet touch ground.

Honey

Carassius auratus auratus

BRONX, NEW YORK

Dinner had just ended and the dishes were stacked in the sink, all except mine. My plate lay before me, empty but for a damp pile of spinach, which I spun in slow spirals with my fork. My eyes paced between the remains of my meal and my father, who watched with a look of silent forbearance, just waiting for me to learn something. Why not the sweetness of corn, I wanted to know, or the lush bite of carrots?— Carrots, of which Cézanne once said, when "freshly observed, will set off a revolution."

It couldn't have been long before the cat came in, but I imagine my attention turned eagerly from the dinner table stalemate to delight in the precious distraction of a new presence in the room: tawny coat, white underbelly, all his familiar softness, postured and prideful. I don't know how long it took for us to realize something was amiss, to register the fiery iridescence of his eyes, the wet fur around his paws, the odd incongruity that hung from his mouth—something more brightly orange than he: a boiled carrot, a wedge of clementine, a crescent of cantaloupe.

But in fact, it was my goldfish that the cat dropped like an offering before us: the wet squish of its body falling to the floor, the splat as it landed, a flash of orange light, limp and lustrous against the white linoleum tile floor. And then the world spiraled into action—

My father, with the one-armed gesture of a swinging Indiana Jones, shooed the cat, scooped up the fish, and motioned to my brother, spritely sidekick, who trailed just a step behind as they disappeared from the kitchen, which had morphed into its own Temple of Doom. Even the overcooked spinach, which had grown cold, turned to a sort of algae on the sea of my plate.

On the floor a thimble-sized splash of pale orange pooled like watercolor. Somewhere beside me I heard the word honey and recognized my mother's careful voice, trying to soothe, trying to decipher the depth of a child's pain. Honey? And I now know it was less a question than an address, not honey as nurtured by bees, but "honey" as in a mother's endearment. But now it is the lasting image of my first bout of grief: the smear left on the tiled floor, part water, part blood, part pearly pulp and scales. If orange were to leave a footprint it would be not juice or nectar but honey. Not so easily wiped away, but thick and lingering, as sweet as it is sticky—

Like Cézanne's carrots, it is not so much about revolution, but about the intricate grace of still life. Not the orange of pet goldfish but the orange crush of first love. Not O'Hara's ORANGES, which turned out to be twelve poems, or prose. In the same way, Goldberg's SARDINES became mingling letters and then a sea of white paint. Or now, because time gessoes the deepest wounds, it is not the goldfish but the linoleum that I see, just the white gleaming tile. Just a small dab of honey.

Later that night, the floor wiped clean, my spinach tossed with the rest of the dinner scraps, we flushed the goldfish down the toilet. All of the family gathered around. I'd like to say that I held the cat in my arms, too, that I had invited him to the service. But it would be weeks of snubbing his purr before I buried my grudge and nuzzled into his warm spots again. My loyal cat, after all, had opened the door to the white space of loss. What injustice! What cruel betrayal! For weeks I would think about heaven, try to imagine it, a faraway room at the end of a tunnel, a porcelain chamber or small empty bowl in the basement of the heart where my goldfish went to rest, joining countless schools and long-lost cousins—

My goldfish, which I ran home to every day to finger flakes of feed over its underwater city of plastic castles and sea ferns and pebbled sand.

I peered into its bowl like a landlocked ingénue pining wrist-deep into its tank, trying to stroke the slippery surface of my small bright ruler, to touch what's close enough to touch but never close enough to hold, in the playground, in the kingdom of deathly fragile dreams—*how terrible orange is, and life!*

I wonder, if there were fewer goldfish, would our hearts not suffer so early through lessons of delicacy and scale? Like an unwatered gill—that mere incision's worth of air—we are as powerless against loss as a goldfish against an eager-to-please housecat.

But then I think that maybe the cat loved the goldfish as much as I did, so much that he wanted to eat her. I myself had wanted to take a spoonful of the kitty, inhale his velvety coat, and nibble his paws. I've since wanted to consume lovers in this way, gnaw on their skin, ingest their bodies, pull them deep inside. But such is lust, not love.

In love we swallow the impulse to devour. We convey affection through gesture and language instead. Similarly, we learn to swallow hatred as if it were a forkful of overcooked greens. It is the swallowing that dignifies compassion. It is the honey that coats the tongue and throat. It is the honey that offers a little sweetness even as it pierces the impeccable royalty of youth. Why not wage a revolution in orange? Why not drip honey along the shallow creases of our gills? Why not invite the greatest persecutors of the heart to the funerals of our friends, and breathe again, through the paper cut of longing?

The B Side

Truth is a burning guitar.
BOB KAUFMAN

I. The Hammer Song

When I was a girl, barely five years old, my father and I held regular recording sessions. In my father's cluttered study I rattled off folk songs and nursery rhymes into a microphone as he played on his classical guitar. A pair of headphones dipped slightly into his Afro and, eyes squinted in concentration, he checked the sound levels on the cassette recorder. Saturday mornings during the fall of '86 were marked by the sound of our indulgence—a blend of high-pitched vocals and acoustic guitar that filled our Bronx apartment.

In the morning, I'd lean over the back of the couch, prop my elbows on the sill of the living room window, and watch the neighborhood stir: the patterns cast on the sidewalk as the morning light changed, the odd habits of our neighbors when they thought they were alone. I watched them closely, as if they were characters in a silent film beyond the window, adding my own narrative, humming the soundtrack.

I'd see one of the neighbors in the front courtyard having just returned from walking her fierce-eyed German shepherd. Her cheeks caked in rouge, the tail end of her cigarette stained Russian red. She bent, mindful of her back, to ash in the flowerbed before heading inside. Across the street, rosy-faced Irish men posted lazily at the chess tables along Greystone Avenue, smoking their morning pipes.

Down the block, kids would soon fill the blacktop to play handball. Later, I'd head out too to assume my perch on the monkey bars, peering over my dangling legs to referee hopscotch on the asphalt below while my mother talked shop with the other young moms. Until then, the streets were quiet—it felt as if the whole block were awaiting our songs.

Before my father woke, I explored the contents of his study. The shelves were lined with records: Joan Baez, Jimi Hendrix, Pete Seeger—we knew most of Seeger's songs by heart. We sang with him when he came to visit the day camp where my mother worked most summers. His metallic banjo rhythms kept time, buoying our voices as we sang near the banks of the Hudson, "This Land Is Your Land," "Had I a Golden Thread," "If I Had a Hammer." Songs that carried meaning well beyond my understanding. I didn't know then that Pete Seeger and Lee Hays wrote "If I Had a Hammer" in 1949, or that it was later revived by Peter, Paul, and Mary in 1962, shortly followed by Sam Cooke's live version at the Copacabana. I didn't know then that the song offered what was, at the time, a radical allegiance to justice first expressed in the labor movement and later in the civil rights struggle of the 1960s. This period in my history was one of singsong simplicity.

In my father's study, I browsed through the 1960s and '70s—rock 'n' roll, Motown recordings, jazz sessions, traditional folk and bluegrass. My father would go on about when Dylan turned electric or how Crosby, Stills, and Nash reunited with Young. He'd talk about protest songs and the power of a well-written lyric. And I'd sit with *Sgt. Pepper* in my lap, tracing the flowers on the cover, wondering if we'd ever sing that way, if we could learn to bend our voices into such uncanny harmonies.

We began each session with an easy warm-up. My father tuned his guitar, humming a note while he plucked each string, now and then tightening a tuning knob. The sound morphed with the twist of his fingers. I swayed with anticipation, twirling a curl of my hair. My father's eyes, deep pools of brown, narrowed as he listened.

At the time, I could only assume my father took "music time" as seriously as I did. If not, he exhibited a remarkable patience. As he tuned, I listened, enjoying the provisional sounds, the same way I liked to lean in close to the record player during the raw whisper between songs, the needle tracing soft warps in the vinyl, its rhythm like a Manhattan taxicab coasting over the rivets along Tenth Avenue.

"Okay," my father said, strumming all six strings. Their sounds merged into one. "Let's hear it." He hummed a note and motioned for me to join him. I cleared my throat and mustered my best vocals. My voice entered the same space as his, as if the two of us had stepped into our own sound booth. We were in tune.

As we moved on to the first song, I glanced up for my cue as my father leaned on the edge of his seat with the first line of "London Bridge Is Falling Down."

The lyrics came like instinct. I fidgeted with the ribbon of my dress. My father, ever casual, wore piped slacks that—though it was well into the 1980s—flared distinctly around his tennis shoes tapping out a beat. He moved seamlessly. Cradling the neck of the guitar in his left hand, he let its hollow body sink to rest on his thigh and strummed again with his right—three fervent chords as we brought the last line to a close: "My ... Fair ... Lady ..."

Every few songs we would take a break from recording. I chattered, disregarding the microphone during my digressions: I wouldn't mind tending a farm where the "Oats and Beans and Barley Grow," though I would never name a dog "Bingo," I told my father, trying to make my five-year-old voice sound mature, subduing, with pursed lips, my inquisitive chime. Also, "I wish I had a watch."

"You wish you had a watch?" my father asked in that half-amused way in which adults echo children.

Quick to recognize an opening, I signaled to my father to hold off on backup and focused on a speedy rendition of "Hickory, Dickory, Dock," *a capella.*

When we hadn't voices left to sing, we'd listen. A handful of cassette tapes were stacked like a cairn by the stereo. They were labeled neatly— my initials, the date—penned in my father's hand the same way he tagged the backs of our photographs, J.H.P. *September, 1986.*

My father leaned his guitar against the wall, waiting for the base to steady before removing his hand from the neck.

I felt my cheeks ball up to my eyes as he handed me a pair of headphones. They haloed my head.

My father reset the tape to play from the beginning. "Listening is the most important part," he would say. The grainy whisper of the guitar strings and the deep-rooted hum of my father's voice tickled my ear. My own voice, so often shy, felt bold.

———

Back then I had no way of knowing to what extent I would grow to value these moments. But on occasion I noticed my mother hovering nearby, taking photographs as we sang, which solidified my suspicion that they were special. I was certain of my father's musical gift. I seemed to sense, too, if vaguely, the indelible appreciation for music that he bestowed on me at an early age.

But it wasn't just the music. My father also taught me the city, and for many years I understood the two as intertwined. Together, we recited the subway stops from Van Cortlandt Park in the Bronx to Union Square in Manhattan and back again; I learned the names of streets and avenues, counted time between the changing traffic lights. We watched *West Side Story* and hummed the melodies of Leonard Bernstein as we passed the chalk-lined basketball courts on Riverside. We saw the musical instruments at the Metropolitan. On the museum steps, we snacked on pretzels and listened to the nearby street drummers playing for change.

I spent much of my childhood believing that life would at some point reveal itself as a string of magically recorded moments. I later realized that music was the only working transmission between my father and me. The memories that are distinct to our relationship relate to the sound of his voice: the stories he told; the songs he sang each night before bed; the way he hummed when he was concentrating, lips slightly parted, his tongue against his teeth.

I don't know, precisely, when things began to change. I remember one day, riding the subway downtown, my brother and I clamored our way to kneel by the window seats as we always did. Propping our elbows on the edge, we peered through the graffiti-etched glass to study the elevated view of Bronx neighborhoods before descending into the tunnels of Manhattan. In my head I practiced the nursery rhymes my father and I would sing—"Farmer Joe," "London Bridge"—my humming muted by the subway's roar. The tunnel lights blurred, keeping time: My . . . Fair . . . Lady. I looked over at my father, who sat calmly, eyes closed, arms crossed on his chest, one foot tapping out a beat. But he didn't sing along.

The Dollhouse

The local newspaper ad read: "Experienced craftsperson wanted . . . excellent pay." The listed telephone number belonged to a woman in Yonkers who had purchased a dollhouse as a gift for her niece—a girl of seven years, same as me—and found herself without the means to properly assemble it. My mother had been searching the classifieds for months, taking odd jobs to make some extra money "for a rainy day."

The forecast promised rain nearly every day that month. The summer of 1989 was marked as much by the acidic scent before a thunderstorm as by the humid swelling of tensions between my parents, whose marriage moved steadily toward collapse. By midsummer, in the form of varying sheets of perforated balsa wood and blueprint instructions, the Granville dollhouse arrived. My mother set to work constructing a mansion in a half-emptied room in our Bronx apartment.

The dollhouse was modeled after the Bedford Falls house in Frank Capra's *It's a Wonderful Life*. When the makings of the Granville arrived, my mother sat looking at her supplies. I knelt beside her and peered over the table where she had laid out the thin slabs of wood, tins of glue, small clamps, and a utility knife.

"How does that song go?" my mother asked, humming a few words about a "very fine house" before turning her attention back to the table. I didn't know then that Graham Nash's "Our House," written about his affair with Joni Mitchell, ran as a looped, almost inescapable, melody in my mother's head that summer. At the time, her humming just lightened the thickness in the air.

I examined the family: four miniature dolls my mother made, painting their muslin faces to resemble each of our own—my mother and father, my older brother and me—stitching a heart at the breast under each felted jumper. *The Family*, I called them, as if needing to feel *the family* as a tangible collective, characters in a scene I might narrate, a play I might one day direct—or simply hold all together in the palm of my hand.

A warm breeze carried the scent of honeysuckle from the neighbor's garden. My mother inhaled and then, worried the humidity might affect the balsa, rose to shut the window. I splayed the dolls like a deck of cards in my hand and asked my mother how big the house would be when it was finished. Studying the blueprint, she said, "We'll have to wait and see."

With slender hands, my mother aligned the thicker slabs of the Granville's foundation. As she sanded the edge of a floor panel, sawdust showered her forearms. She still had the frame of her high school days, though no longer the mousy blonde bob. She still stared off with the lost wonder of those teenage years, the same strength of conviction waiting to bud from the flowers in her hair.

I looked down at the dolls in my lap. They were near perfect, though too small to bear the minor details that compose the portrait of a family. My father's brown skin and black hair; the glassy blue of my mother's eyes, the pale softness of her skin; or my brother and me, filling in the spectrum of color in between.

My parents married in 1976. As college dropouts and art school graduates, they left their Pennsylvania suburbs for a quick stay outside Boston, where my brother was born, and then found sanctuary in New York, where, in the fall of 1982, I was born into the hands of a midwife in a maternity center on Ninety-Second and Madison. At the time—before she landed a job as a high school secretary—my mother worked as a seamstress and held a closing shift at McDonald's. My father, having recently finished a stint in seminary, was enrolled in a master's program at Columbia University, because somewhere between art and religion he believed he might find his doctrine.

By the time I was five, we had moved to a small corner of the Bronx, due north of Manhattan, into a two-family house built into a hill.

My mother fixed the garden out back, brought home paint swatches from the hardware store, painted each room a different color based on the allure of its name: *Shrimp Toast, Celadon Cloud, Rusted Persimmon*. We danced barefoot on the patio when it rained. My mother wrote poetry and waited for the Solstice; my father composed music on his guitar and painted in the attic; my brother and I grew up sewing patches on our corduroys, composting our food scraps, and worshipping Cat Stevens and Sweet Honey in the Rock.

My parents scraped just enough together to toggle between urban streets and natural landscapes. Summers meant sun tea and rock candy, salamanders along the creek beds of New England, sea glass and cowry shells on the shores of the Atlantic. In winter we went west to my grandfather's ranch in Tucson, where we baked fudge on Christmas and weighed horse feed at dawn.

But New York grounded us. We lived on the line where the enclave of Riverdale dissolves into the massive borough of the Bronx. Tucked below the Westchester suburbs, the neighborhood is bookended by the Hudson and two-way traffic on Broadway. Orthodox Jewish families stroll the tree-lined streets on Saturdays, while the Irish bagpipes sound off a game of hurling at Gaelic Park. On 238th Street, old couples with their Sunday hats and swollen ankles line up outside the diner for the early morning bus to Atlantic City. Slow-moving trains creak along the elevated subway platform, heading one stop north to retire in the train yard near Van Cortlandt Park, which, on summer afternoons, pulses with salsa or merengue and the smell of backyard barbeque—enough sweetness in the air to make your mouth water for days.

John F. Kennedy once owned a house on Independence Avenue. The women in the Laundromat gossiped about Ed Sullivan's apartment in The Whitehall as if it were John Lennon in The Dakota. And, though it meant little then—a real TV man in the same building as the neighborhood dentist—it confirmed my suspicions that the closer to the river my brother and I rode our bicycles, the larger the houses grew, and the richer the people inside. But our attentions were tuned in elsewhere.

"Turn that up, would you?" my mother would say, motioning a dish-watered hand toward the NPR broadcast on the kitchen counter. Just as my father's voice bellowed each night from the living room, reminding us kids to *keep it down* during *MacNeil/Lehrer*.

In the summer of 1989, downtown city politics was a spiraling staircase toward chaos and evictions. Tenants were battling landlords. Mom-and-pop establishments were being bullied by boutiques. Nearly a year had passed since the riots in Tompkins Square Park—a violent showdown between warring tenants, ad hoc activists, the city's fearless fringe, and the NYPD after the mayor dispatched city police to enforce a curfew, running off the homeless and squatters who, in the sweltering heat, had taken up residence in the East Village park. And again, that summer a year later, the city made plans to dismantle the encampments known as Tent City. At the time, of course, I was ignorant of these details, but I had gleaned just enough from newspaper images and radio news to sense that somewhere, not far away, things were awry, that we had reason for concern.

———

Squatting before her worktable, my mother installed a banister along what would be the Granville's front porch. She was dressed down in the heat, her T-shirt hanging loose around her neck and billowing over her cutoff shorts. Her ears, normally adorned with beaded earrings, were bare, her silvery hair wrapped neatly away in a faded bandanna.

I inhaled the smell of wood glue. My mother handed me a scrap of balsa wood. With its narrow edge, I scrawled my name in the sawdust that blanketed the floor. My mother reached down to untwist a strap of my overalls. She knew how much I loved it there, with her, with the Granville. But I was careful not to be a bother. Something in her silence that summer suggested that she needed to build the house alone.

Instead I became obsessed with the spirit of the Granville. We all did for a while. When we had nothing to talk about, we talked about the dollhouse. At dinner my father would ask how it was coming along. My mother issued progress reports as we filled our milk glasses and passed the salt.

"Whoever gets the dollhouse should paint it camouflage," my brother once said.

To which I responded, "That's ridiculous," as if knowing then that the mansion's refinement was fit for a scene of a Fitzgerald novel, where the parvenus of Long Island Sound gathered by the shore. I hoped it would belong to a girl with a wagging ponytail, pressed dresses, and enough sensibility to wallpaper the interior—dreams interrupted only by my mother's voice of reason. "Let's just remember," she said, "the house will belong to another family when it's complete."

Some of my friends lived in big houses with parents who entertained in distant dining rooms and checked in every hour. In our cramped apartment we tripped over one another. While I recognized what fun it might be to slide down a banister into a spacious foyer, or close the door to my own bedroom, I filtered between such envies and a distinct pride in our family's differences—the comfort of our close quarters, each of us no more than a name call away. But it didn't always feel that way.

In the summer of 1989, it seemed my parents hardly crossed paths, as though the humidity had swelled not just the balsa wood but also an invisible rift between them. My brother offered far-fetched ideas of a secluded base camp for his G.I. Joe action figures. I countered with imaginings of a house filled with pint-sized debutantes and miniature armoires. As well-loved children sheltered by our youth, we bickered in oblivion, filling the hollow silence as we played with our vegetables.

That summer, during a brief respite from the heat, my mother knelt in the yard, staking tomato plants along the stoned wall of our garden. I watched our neighbor Frank—old, Italian, with kind eyes and a widowed heart—tend a cucumber vine that crawled along the fence between our yards. Frank's house was built farther up on the hill. I rarely caught sight of him from level ground.

Next door, on the same hillside where Waldo Avenue and Dash Place meet at a sharp bend, lived another family with children. Their house, built of stone with wide-planked mahogany floors, creaked when we played.

"That house is very old," my mother said. "Years ago it was probably the main house. And these," she motioned a handful of weeds toward our house and then Frank's, "probably belonged to the grown children." In the nineteenth century, she explained, the Riverdale section of the Bronx was an estate district where Manhattan moguls built their country homes.

"Back then this was considered the country," she said.

"So we live in the daughter's house?" I asked.

"Not exactly. The entire house likely belonged to the daughter. Our apartment may have been the maid's quarters."

In some pockets of the neighborhood, historic manors remained more or less intact. But with the advent of apartment living, several streets were transformed to create a modern-day hodgepodge of distinguished Georgian and Tudor revivals from the twentieth century, prewar co-ops, luxury condos, and midrange housing projects.

We lived in the maid's quarters. I tried to imagine where we fit in on the architectural scale, just how we measured up in the neighborhood, in life.

In an early scene in It's a Wonderful Life, George Bailey and Mary Hatch sing an old tune before they stop in front of the Granville. The dilapidated house towers large in the background. The young couple nearly shares a kiss before backing away from each other in a classic moment of awkward shyness. George says: "Okay then, I'll throw a rock at the old Granville house and try to break some glass." To which Mary is quick to protest: "It's full of romance, that old place," adding with breathy sincerity, "I'd like to live in it one day." They each make a wish and hurl stones at the windows. George has a whole list of wishes. Mary has only one. But she doesn't dare tell.

On one of the sweltering days in the summer of 1989, I asked my mother, "If you had three wishes, what would they be?" She stood sweeping matchsticks and sawdust from the floor. Then, propping her chin on the broomstick, she considered the question. The dollhouse sat on the nearby table. Each day it had taken more form. I circled it, peering into its skeletal frame, its interior nooks and doorways, its zigzagging staircases. My mother joined me, crouching to inspect the innards of her creation. On opposite sides we could see each other by way of the cavernous foyer. Small vertical beams soon to be walls hid the full image of her face, like the rosewood grating of a confessional.

"I would wish for a house like this one," I whispered.

Through the Granville I saw only my mother's eyes, sharply blue as the light turned and the air braced for rain. I stood and ran around to where she was kneeling on the floor.

"I also wish that I had a cat," I said. "One who goes in circles before he sits. Like this—" I rolled my hands into pawed fists and kneaded them gently into her thigh. My mother laughed and squeezed my hands.

Satisfied at least with her smile, I headed off to find my brother. Before I got far, I stopped to listen: the broom swept against the floor, keeping rhythm as my mother, left alone, hummed an incessant song.

By the end of the summer, the Granville was complete. My father carried the house out to the garden and placed it on a stool. My mother posed for a photograph. Her expression was stiff but proud, one arm draped awkwardly over the shingled roof.

My father tinkered with the Pentax, showing my brother how to focus the lens. My mother leaned down to me and whispered, "Go and bring the family," fingering the curls at the nape of my neck. She said it too—the family—referring to the four miniature dolls, those characters in our unwinding script.

After retrieving the dolls I propped them one by one around the exterior of the house—my father and brother on the second-floor balcony, my own doll bent to sit on the porch steps, my mother propped at a slant in the threshold behind me. They were the perfect size for an otherwise unfurnished home.

After the photographs, I collected the dolls and stood them up in the front pocket of my overalls. Leaning back into my mother, I pulled her arms around my neck and we watched my father carry the dollhouse away. I realized then how much my mother hated to see it go. Oddly, I don't remember feeling too disturbed watching the Granville move on. Perhaps, because my mother had prepared me for the moment, it seemed inevitable. Or maybe I was more concerned with what might come next. In the crease of her elbow the faint smell of patchouli oil, sawdust, and sweat turned to the metallic scent of rain.

———

Two years passed between the dollhouse and "the end," but it was that humid summer of 1989, the rain, the Granville that most capture the memory of my parents' divorce. After the dollhouse there was relative normalcy in our home. Sometimes I wonder how little I remember of those years. Or rather, how well my parents masked the budding divide between them. The weeks and months read as a period of prolonged silence. We grew accustomed.

My father spent more and more time holed away in the attic with his guitar. My mother took night workshops at a nearby city college to hone her poetry and make new friends. I entered the second grade and assumed a dose of elementary-level diversion: pottery classes, extended recess, Laura Ingalls Wilder novels. And likewise, more grappling concepts: friendship circles, boys, pop music. I came to ignore the hushed interactions, the closed doors behind which my parents, young and disappointed, were negotiating their marriage.

I was nine years old when, two years after the Granville dollhouse but an equally hot and humid evening, my father's clenched fist came down against the half-cleared kitchen table. My brother and I sat in the living room watching the changing glow of an old film playing on TV.

We listened as our parents argued in the kitchen. My father's barreling voice and my mother's shrill cries carried, not as decipherable words, but as noise that filled every corner of our apartment.

I pinched at my brother and whispered, "What are they saying?"

He swatted at my hand and snapped at me to shut up. And then almost immediately said, "I'm sorry," and inched closer as a cascade of dishes sounded down the hall. We sat cross-legged with our backs together the way we often did, as if indeed camouflaged. I tried to move even closer, but my dress had risen under me and, in the heat, my bare legs stuck to the floor. A gust of air entered the living room window and boiled around us.

Next, I remember my parents crouched on the floor beside us. In the tangle of their arms, my father stroked my hair and kneaded my brother's shoulder, assuring us that "things would be better now." His voice was heavy, smooth like tar. My mother wept apologies in my ear.

We ate at the kitchen table for weeks, setting our plates over the crack in the white Formica finish left by my father's fist, which it turned out, had also been broken that day. We tried to ignore the fractured surface. My father's hand was in a cast for weeks while he moved into his own apartment up the street.

I knew from a young age that my parents were different. They expected more from the world. But their politics were not manifest in picket lines. I wasn't thrown on my father's back attending protest rallies downtown. I have no lasting images of my mother with bullhorn or soapbox amid a swarming crowd. In our house, society's underbelly surfaced as protagonists of my mother's poems or the drawings that hung above my father's drafting table. In one, a black boy peers up at a mounted police officer, a small stone clenched in the fist behind his back. For years, I imagined it as a still frame from a motion picture, and wondered what might have happened next—if the ideals of art and love could trump reality; if I could run away with a boy like that, all patience and courage, and live off morals and a handful of stones.

My parents, I have no doubt, set out to build something solid. But by the time I was seven I had learned about impermanence. Just as the Granville, adorned in decadent possibility, would come and go, my parents were architects of what could only be a short-lived wonderland.

In the mid-1990s, while New York City's homeless still resided in the streets, news of Giuliani's crackdown aired on the radio. Life went on. But we were all changed. My father stopped writing protest ballads on his guitar; my mother no longer gathered wildflowers along the side of the road; my brother and I settled into the routine shuffle between our parents' apartments.

———

Most people know the Bedford Falls house in Capra's film, as well as the story of George Bailey, who in his moment of despair is visited by an angel and given a glimpse of the meaning of life. But these are only the superficial details—the ones I would have gleaned from the film as a girl. As the film ensues we learn of George Bailey as a boy who aspires to design buildings and construct cities, of his compassion for the working class as he battles the most abominable landlord in the country, of the tension in his marriage, of the Granville Mansion, the run-down structure that houses their dreams.

Perhaps the greatest gift the angel offers George Bailey is the reel of a life that might have been had various events never occurred. But to some extent we can gain perspective on our own lives only by revisiting the scenes not as they may have been, but as they were, or at least as close to it as the lasting images allow.

A week or two after my parents' decisive fight, my mother knelt on the floor over a splayed newspaper, packing a box of my father's things. She stopped to skim a news story before clipping the article. The headline said something about bulldozing in the shantytowns. By then Mayor Dinkins held the reins of the city as police in riot gear escorted men and women from abandoned buildings and East Village squats. The half-faded picture in the newspaper showed a woman in a wheelchair out on the street.

My mother said, "The city doesn't know how to handle its homeless," and I nodded, trying to emulate her quiet scorn, which is something I have yet to fully master.

My mother pinned the clipping into her notebook against the handwritten elegy she had penned earlier that day. I studied the woman's face in the newsprint, photographed minutes after her eviction. Her expression held resentment, fear. Her belongings lay piled in a nearby shopping cart. A cat sat close in her lap. At once this woman had become the heroine in my script. The newspaper caption read "Pixie Louise"—not quite an angel but a fairy—and quoted her describing her home made of wood, metal pipe beams, and a tarp cover, saying, "there was nothing shoddy about where we lived." With her crooked wandlike fingers and vacant gaze, she both embodied and demolished the illusion that once held us—its fancy cornices and wrap-around porch, constructed precisely to plan, smooth but weightless—a dollhouse, after all. A structure not built for us.

The B Side

II. Somewhere

Nearly thirty minutes into the 1961 film adaptation of *West Side* Story, Natalie Wood as Maria argues with Anita over the cut of her dress. Soon they will be at the neighborhood dance—the Puerto Rican boys are already on their way to pick them up—and when Maria slides into the iconic white dress with a trim red sash, she falls rapt, spellbound by the promise of her first night out in America. The music heightens as she twirls in front of a full-length mirror. Her body blurs à la mid-century special effects. The background darkens around her colorful haze, fades, and then refocuses again on a gymnasium full of Jets and Sharks dancing the mambo with their girls. Each time I've seen the film, the moment, despite its Technicolor excess, rings true: transitions are a whirlwind; trying to belong in a star-crossed world can lead to a dizzying spiral away from what we know.

When I was nine and my father moved into his own apartment, it felt for years as if the music had stopped. By the 1990s, when I entered high school, the details of my father began to fade as he seemed to grow less and less involved in the daily aspects of my adolescence. Only rarely did I see him pick up his guitar. To be fair, I had limited time to observe his behavior as my brother and I assumed the weekly schedule—Tuesdays, Thursdays, alternate weekends—of many nomadic children of divorce. Perhaps, on occasion, he did finger-pick along to the jazz instrumentals of a few contemporaries: Chick Corea on piano, Al Di Meola's electric guitar, some early Jean-Luc Ponty on violin before he, too, resorted to electric fusion. My father burned incense in his apartment, slept often, and added several New Age records to his collection—their synthetic timbres like ghosts of an instrumental past. Meanwhile, I scoured the secondhand shops for old rock and blues albums of Janis Joplin and Nina Simone, Dylan, too. Some nights at my father's apartment, I sat paging through *Othello* or *A Tale of Two Cities* for English class, thinking about the French revolution in London and Paris, eventually returning to the Beats—memorizing verses of "Howl" and "Kaddish"—while eyeing my father, who sat glued to the television. At sixteen, in the chaos of adolescence, I hoped for something to hold on to, like the comfort of a childhood rhyme or a timeless folk song resurrected. The space around us once filled with music felt vacant, still.

One night I emerged from my bedroom and found my father in front of the television.

"Just in time," he said motioning to the screen where the *Double Jeopardy!* category listed "Rock 'n' Roll."

I grabbed his guitar off a stand in the far corner of the room, blew lightly at the film of dust on the top edge, and sat on the couch, palming the cool wooden face as my father chimed answers over the on-air contestants.

"This guy is incredible," he said pointing to the screen where a middle-aged man, clad in a tweed blazer and crimson bow tie, stood grinning behind a podium. My father was wrapped in a dark flannel robe. His eyeglasses rested on the bridge of his nose. I remember thinking how old he looked then. He no longer bore the height and build of his youth, when he'd held me in his arms, his guitar slung around his back, singing "Blackbird" in my ear as I fingered his spongy black hair.

That year in school we studied civil disobedience, and this history teacher, whom I was crushing on hard, told me about the poet Bob Kaufman. After that, as if a fire were lit, I needed to know my father's story more than ever before. How he became so staunchly antiwar, how he used to play protest songs in downtown cafés. I wanted to ask about the day he received his draft card, about who shot Kennedy, who ended the Vietnam War—and did any of it really matter? Except that somewhere in San Francisco a poet was vowing silence, refused to be a citizen of speech until the war came to an end—how it's a wonder he never lost his voice, just kept the rhythm in his chest, somewhere beneath his beatnik poncho and flares. For a moment, at the start of a commercial break, I thought I might catch my father's attention, but he waved his hand.

"One minute," he said, leaning to grab the remote control on the coffee table between us.

The screen cut to the blue *Jeopardy!* backdrop of the stage. The familiar theme music chimed over audience applause. My father waited for the cue of a commercial break to pause his videocassette recorder.

"I like to revisit the questions sometimes," he explained. "When you listen again, you learn things you didn't catch the first time."

I looked down at the guitar in my lap and traced my fingers along its strings, listening to the eerie whistle of steel against my skin, like a slowing train car or the call of a seagull lost offshore.

———

In April 1968, Diana Ross went live on Johnny Carson's *Tonight Show* and sang a version of Leonard Bernstein's composition "Somewhere"—the same song Maria and Tony sing just after gang rivals Riff and Bernardo are killed at the rumble. The song had been a staple in the Supremes' lounge act, but that particular performance took place a day after the assassination of Martin Luther King. In the middle of the song Ross stopped singing, as she often did, to address the audience. But instead of her usual interlude on romance, she incited the spiritual hymn from King's "I Have a Dream" speech. Ross's performance met with some skepticism by critics who considered it a pop-diva-turns-political kind of moment, and was often dismissed by the press as a superficial political gesture. But in old video recordings, you can see the unease in Ross's body. You can hear the emotional overwhelm in her voice—a voice that is sleepy and sad and stumbles slightly over the lines, a voice that, in its impromptu uncertainty, carries grace.

My father had become little more than a collage of sparse details, a set of trivia—a game show category himself—that loosely coincided with milestones in the history of American music. In 1956, when rockabilly classics dominated the radio waves, my father, just five years old, picked up his first guitar, and for a long time he never let it go. That same year, he and his sister sent in a mail-order coupon for a pair of Elvis Presley sideburns. In 1964, when the Beatles arrived in the States and my father turned thirteen, he and his grandmother sang "Can't Buy Me Love" as they danced in the muddy yard behind his childhood home. The year he was drafted to Vietnam, 1970, was two years after the assassinations of King and Kennedy, the nationwide race riots, and antiwar demonstrations; it was two years since *The White Album* had topped the charts and Diana Ross, live on TV, had tried to make sense of all the tragedy. But my father never went to war.

Before I had a moment to question again, he shifted his gaze to the television and reset the machine. I slouched back, the guitar flat against my thighs, listening to the variations as I pinched and plucked each string.

A *Double Jeopardy!* category flashed on screen. "Literary Quotations," he said. "Right up your alley."

Pressing against the guitar frets, I felt the finely ribbed strings leaving grooves in my fingertips, and the aching regret that I had never learned to play. Because had I learned, I might simply hole up in my room and strum myself the chords of the folk songs and nursery rhymes we once loved.

"Do you want to play?" I asked, holding the guitar out, obscuring the view of Alex Trebek.

My father shrugged and blew into his teacup. As his attention turned back to the contestants, I lowered the guitar to my lap again.

Without holding any notes, I strummed hard. The open strings buzzed wildly out of tune. My father glanced over to me and raised an eyebrow. I left the guitar on the couch and walked back to my room. No Technicolor twirling. No special effects. But something in me transitioning nonetheless.

———

My father's past, as I understood it then, was full of holes and unanchored facts. What I did know about him maintained my regard for him as a father and exposed a unique strength: he was born to rural poverty; he never knew his own father; as the oldest of three children, he cared for his mother and younger siblings; and as a young man in the 1960s, he learned to play the tuba and traveled Europe as the sole black student in a marching band.

Over time, my father became more of a concept than a man, more of an acquaintance than a father. In the same way that he rescreened his game show, I reread my books. I may have wished for a catalyst to address the estrangement between us, but in my teenage sulk, I grew equally distant. By the time I was eighteen and graduated from high school, there were no sounds beyond those of halting taxicabs and unfazed pedestrians, loud-mouthed neighbors, and smooth-talking players. The sounds of a childhood city, like a folk song I once loved, now seemed abrasive. I had grown out of the dress shop or perhaps out of the dress itself; I couldn't be sure amid all of my turning and whirling, my spiraling toward somewhere far away.

Mirror, Mirror

Flying—or, not yet in the air but staring impatiently through the port-hole of the Boeing window while the attendant closes the overhead bins during cross-check—it comes to me: a line from an old diary. The first in a series of entries addressed to Leonardo da Vinci when I was seven, or perhaps eight, when I would have called it a journal—somehow older-sounding, a little more mature:

> It's true; it's all backwards to them anyhow.

Except that when I wrote the words, I began from the right side of the page. With my left hand, I reversed each letter's form, aligning the letters neatly atop the page's faint lines. I moved swiftly toward the center binding—the people's margin—that place where we learn, when we are small, to begin.

But it didn't have to be that way. Da Vinci knew this. His notebooks, now stored in climate-controlled libraries and vaults, were scrawled in mirror-image cursive. His works bear inscriptions like primitive forms of cipher, Islamic calligraphy, or Samaritan script. The kind of imprints found on ancient tablets and gilded parchment—the Torah, the Koran, the Book of Kells. Maybe this is where my obsession with holy books began, why I thought I might write one someday, its pages all beginnings and endings, footnotes and failures, about a girl who played in sprinklers while loving Heraclitus. (Or, rather, rinsed off in hydrants while lusting after da Vinci.) Leonardo—

> the most clever of them all.
> the most clever of them all.

Around this time, just before the divorce, I remember hearing my parents, when they still shared citizenry in love and other illusions, discussing da Vinci's methods, musing over his madness in the same breath as his genius. And I admired, even then, the conflict in their tone, as much as I may have recognized the same inflection as they addressed my reticence, shyness, and odd behavior. A tone not extended to my older brother, local superhero, his cape tucked away with the magic set he brought out when he performed card tricks for our friends. He kept secrets like Houdini or, rather, some Jedi-mind-tricking Karate Kid, who carried the best beat box in the sixth grade, back when such titles held cachet. He has been a master of mirage ever since he began practicing his disappearing acts in high school, stashing his lies, along with the booze and stolen goods, in the trapdoor of his closet.

Second-born and sister, I was the strange and silent sidekick. No stockpile of trophies stowed beneath my bed, though my mattress hid a few miniature jars with an alchemist's concoction of Old Spice and Barbasol, baking soda and cinnamon, a dash of glitter, my mother's shampoo—love potions and "pretty brews" I kept safe for later. I took pride in knowing that my middle name held the symmetry of a palindrome, that the mirror image of certain words was as heartbreaking as the original. How mood swings with the weight of a boom—a never even palindrome, a pendulum that might near stillness but not quite hang level. Or the hidden pleasure of a word like bid—because what greater stakes might a word contain than appearing, forward and backward, exactly the same? Like siblings sharing DNA, how many words grow apart in opposite direction? The way loot is the wild-mannered sister to the ever-skilled, ever-talented brother tool. He—

the most gifted child by far.
the most gifted child by far.

Perhaps this is why, while my brother and his friends waged b-boy battles in the yard, high-tops swivel-kicking over our mother's flower-beds, I was content to disappear and visit the neighbors. On days when the boy next door had his weekly Greek lesson, I sat with his mother listening from their kitchen. I tried to record the words I knew on the back side of a grocery list that his mother placed before me while she prepared us coffee in tiny porcelain cups, which contained fortunes and futures that she read from the pattern left in the grounds. I was content, too, to tag along after school on the days when my best friend had Hebrew school, to practice the alphabet—a twenty-two-letter script of consonants—starting with our pencils at the right side of the page. Such order was akin to levity in the otherwise spiraling world. Some nights I would linger on our doorstep and listen for the man downstairs we rarely saw and only sometimes heard, whom I imagined a watchmaker or inventor, a connoisseur of model planes. Something like that: smart and neat and quiet. Or sometimes it was enough to head inside early, prop the TV antenna in order to catch the nightly lotto numbers or Sajak's *Wheel of Fortune* (all that luck and puzzle spinning 'round!), or settle on reruns of *Nature*, trying to decipher each kingdom, phylum, genus, order—behind all the static, while searching for pictures like cloud patterns and constellations in the sky.

Not long ago, on a red-eye from New York to Rome, I listened to an old woman sitting in the row behind me talk about her granddaughter and mathematics—how, although most children favor addition, she's quite fond of subtraction. This, one of her more "precocious quirks." I wonder what that means, her fondness for subtraction, and then I have one of those moments when I think, This will find its way into your dreams, like a splinter or a needle prick. And, inevitably, it does. I envy this anonymous girl, profound erasure artist. I wonder what she knows that the rest of us don't, as she scrapes her knees in the playground, maybe fights with a brother or a stepsister. How much will she figure out with her love of deduction, solving for x, as she will?—X, one of few letters appearing one and the same in its reflection. Maybe that's why cartographers chose x for treasure. Maybe x will always mark the division between her and them, whoever *they* are, as if a magic mirror revealing the "takeaway" of childhood.

Finding explanation in scientific terms is easy, just as it is easy to find definition in a dictionary. But where is the meaning in that? Studies show that mirror writing is a question of atypical language organization, a product of a genetic trait closely associated with left-handedness, ambidexterity, synesthesia, and other oddities that, at the time, made everything seem—different. The pattern of inheritance is not entirely clear, but evidence suggests that the ability is passed through the X chromosome, regardless of which parent may have carried it. I imagine my parents—non–mirror writers, I've since confirmed—and the look

they must have shared over my encrypted pages, as I scribbled away
unaware.

Could I have known then of da Vinci's paranoia? (And was that really,
as some historians would have us believe, what made him scrawl in
reverse?) Or was this my expression of a girlhood crush? Perhaps,
because I was eight, I would have called him my role model, fifteenth-
century polymath that he was. How else can I explain how I swooned
over a reproduction of *The Vitruvian Man* that hung in the living room,
the figure superimposed in two positions, one inhabiting the circle, the
other the square? Love-struck by this canon of proportion, smitten by
da Vinci's precisely rendered sketches, I paged through my parents' art
books, where graphite and conté marked his architectural and anatomical forms: *Designs for a flying machine, Study for the head of Leda or Saint Anne,*
or the *Trivulzio Monument, Study of concave mirrors of differing curvatures, Study
of water passing obstacles and falling—*

who is the greatest dreamer of them all?

who is the greatest dreamer of them all?

I believe da Vinci's was not a mind wracked by compulsive mistrust
but a mind brimming and at work. For my part, I was no Renaissance
child, no budding whiz kid with genius to protect. And had I something stored in the musty scented pages to keep safe, surely the black
cat silhouette on the cover of my lock-'n'-key diary was sufficient vault.
Instead, I wrote and read back the words, my eyes skipping right to left
along the letterforms, not once consulting a mirror, not daring to seek
their reflection. While I craved the encryption, it was the expediency of
expression that fed me—my own *Nocturne for the Left Hand*—free of the
smudge that branded my schoolwork for years or the awkward tightness
of words smothered by my sleeve. Like in a symbolist composition, the
words carried clarity, one piece of the puzzle I could control, protect,
and practice, devising my own style where each reversed letter carried
a note, soft and tuned and mine.

Those days I grew suspicious of magic school buses and fairy tales
(even those Brothers Grimm) and traded in fantasy for proportion.
The astrological scale I was born under tipping daily just as everything
around me seemed to: the landlady who invited me into her kitchen,
a palace of warm honey and baklava, could in an instant yell with the
wicked breath of ouzo and gin that it was time to go home. The quiet

neighbor, as it turns out, was not consumed by time machines or model planes but was something of a huntsman, tinkering with explosives, constructing pipe bombs beneath my bedroom, which was revealed one sunny school day when we came home to police bagging evidence and escorting him away.

who holds the greatest secrets of us all?

Years later I no longer have the diligence to keep a regular journal—and if I did, I would call it a diary—somehow more transparent, forthright, perhaps even naive. But when daydreaming takes hold, my hand still travels to the right margin of the page, as if propelled by a flying machine toward that familiar reversal. My mirrored shorthand becomes a gliding carpet or a worldly wardrobe, turning a page back in time to visit a girl I once knew, who gazes at me—equal parts longing and disappointment—waiting for some explanation for all the immaculate confusion, all the apples and poisons put before us.

Are my reversals the result of a stubborn nostalgia—a precedent I set out like a tea set, or a trunk of dress-up clothes, and never fully put away? Maybe I'm excited by eccentricity, aroused by the peculiar and the queer. I once slept with a man who collected palindromes, which could have been a spark between us, until I realized he also collected women. The same boy next door had ten letters and four syllables in his Greek name, which I would write repeatedly, forward and backward in my notebooks, oblivious to the sideways glances from my friends, just as I might have missed the one raised eyebrow my brother and father and mother all exchanged over the dinner table—their own special trait—when I said things "out of left field."

I remember trying to explain how numbers are colors—three like yellow, four cool like blue—or how certain words made me itch, gave my body a kind of ache. I remember seeing the faces around me turn, as if delighting in a foreign film in which every time the beloved supporting role steps into the frame, the subtitles jumble and fade, like an x drawn in the sand, above some long lost chromosome no one ever knew would surface so boldly.

Such digressions (words and their colors, spatial relations, sounds) I learned to keep stored, private, recorded in an almanac of riddle and wonder. And now I often think, *so much worry for such a small* girl—everything all backward in the quest to belong, everything needing to be counted, codified:

The steps that cut through the hills of our Bronx neighborhood, I climbed two at a time, so I might make it to the top with breath left; all the cracks and lines in the sidewalk I avoided so as not to break my mother's back or my own fragile spine. So I might sleep at night without recording my pulse, listening for signs of panic, even the slightest turbulence in what should have been the plucky rhythm and dramatic consistency of a ten-year-old heart, wishing for some real elixir that would put me at ease.

Maybe then I would have spent more time with the other girls, watching the boys play wall ball or stickball, stoopball or war, as we huddled clandestinely by the courtyard's chain-link fence, confessing our crushes, wondering if we would ever be pretty enough (and who, really, was the greatest belle of our ball?), as we braided each other's hair and spit-shined our Keds so the soles glared white like snow.

I'm beginning to realize I am fond of subtraction, too. It is similar to wiping dust from a record as it spins and hearing the sound clear, or cleaning out the kitchen drawer on a Sunday afternoon just to see what's inside, to recognize how little we actually need: scissors, a flashlight, a spare set of keys, so we can be the sleuths and cryptographers, aviators and excavators of our own design, digging backward until once upon a time there we are again.

And maybe that says something about why I took to charcoal in college after scraping by in mathematics with a final paper on phi and the golden mean, the first draft written in longhand, half in reverse. By the next semester I had transferred to life drawing so I could feel the smooth grain of charcoal against the page, erasing the blocks of black into a gradient of gray and down to the clean page, where I outlined the contours, the cheeks and chin of the Pietà, the Mona Lisa, *La belle ferronnière*—yes, there she is!—her image projected as a fair queen against a curtain.

It's easy to find beauty in solitude, just as it is easy to find misfortune in loneliness. But where is the reason in that? Where is the margin between the two? I keep thinking how one morning I will get out of bed and things will feel different, that my skin won't be so porous, won't wear like a gown I'm still waiting to grow into, that I won't so easily cringe at the color or texture of things or the sound and shape of the words for those things. Instead, maybe I'll wake up to a call from my brother and he will no longer be among the list of brilliant strangers. He'll be shuffling his cards and telling me about the latest trick he's learned, how it's all "smoke and mirrors," as I peel back a newspaper and scan the latest headlines: *World reaches unanimous vote on new alphabet. Long lost da Vinci notebook suspected to lie beneath the Trivulzio monument. Miraculous descendant of Heraclitus born to teenage parents in Greece—*

what has the world come to, after all?

And then there will be nothing left to do but marvel at invention: the French press or lamplight, colanders and cutlery, a window screen, the fire escape. Even a low-flying airplane headed east over the Atlantic, crossing invisible longitudes where unhinged imagination enters the time zone of abnormality, where daydreams translate into dysfunction, where from the very beginning we've reserved our coach-class seats in the exit row and agreed to come of age over the ocean. Stewards of sadness, we stow longing away as if it were a stutter or tic we've outgrown. In the same way we learn to distrust happily ever after, or odd reclusive neighbors, yet save compassion for the young and the old, though they are no less disillusioned than the lovelorn or the fanatic: The old veteran who spent days at his window, ogling the breasts of women who passed by and harboring hatred for the Japanese, still asked daily after the girl upstairs, who rewrites lines of nothing but her name, as torn and crumpled paper scatters the floor. The landlady who piled her empty bottles in the trash bin outside must have known that I would count them, repeatedly, until I was late for school, where I charted on an invisible x–y axis the scale of her sadness, trying to draft a formula for forgetting, to concoct an antidote to grief.

If only I could write in this space forever. If only I could return to the glass coffin where p resembles q, where b becomes d, where U and I remain intact. Except maybe it's not the secrecy or order that is saving me anymore, not so much the letters or the words but the uncharted margins, the outdated virtues of common things such as fountain pens and telegrams, fine stationery and wax seals, which are not in the least necessary but feel elegant and classy—comforts amid chaos. Like ordering cocktails in the sky from tiny bottles, sipping a macchiato in a quaint café, tossing pennies at Trevi Fountain, posting a letter from the Vatican. Maybe that is what this really is: a letter that holds a mirror to a message I want to write, seal with a kiss, and send to the strange little girl who loves subtraction, the one I know only through the voice behind my seat, and I would write *How brave you are!* and ask what she knows about the future, if subtraction is a long road toward solitude, if *minus equals loss*. The way backward feels synonymous with the most intimate of codes, the way all of life is an enchanted spell we may never come out from under. Is this—

the fairest truth of all?

Or maybe we'll go on not knowing any answers, keep trying to reverse ourselves, erase the parts of us that don't quite fit as the reflection multiplies *ad infinitum*, a word that itself feels wrought with blue and suggests a bright but thinning air. Preparing for takeoff, I secure my seat belt and tray table, and the flight attendant, wielding an oxygen mask like a tasseled wand, mimes an encrypted message of safety, procedure, and the commercial flying machine pushes back and takes to the sky.

The B Side

III. *Blackbird*

When I was in my early twenties and living south of Denver, Colorado—
which was not quite San Francisco but the sky was big and open just
the same—I got in the habit of visiting a Baptist church downtown,
slinking into the back pews unseen, just to see a boy, no more than
nine years old, sing "His Eye Is on the Sparrow." At that point I thought
nothing could top notable performances of that song by Ethel Waters,
Mahalia Jackson, even Lauryn Hill and Tanya Blount, but something
about this boy had me captivated.

That same spring my father sent me a compilation of our old recordings, nearly a year's worth of cassette tapes dubbed and condensed into
a single, slick CD. The small package was addressed with my initials in
the same fluid hand he'd used to label the tapes.

That morning, before the package arrived, I had taken my coffee by
the window and watched the paths of campus fill with students dragging their feet to the dining hall. I listened to the brisk stampede of
the cross-country team cutting across the quad and the lazy hum of
a bicycle over the stone campus paths as I lit a cigarette and, barefoot
and a little bit hung over, tried to balance on a skateboard a boy had
left by my bed.

On the cover of the album my father had fashioned an old photograph of me nestled into his big leather chair, same bare legs and bony
feet. His guitar filled my lap, my arms rested on the glazed wood of its
hollow form.

As the cross-country team circled back, returning from their mountain drills, I still sat with the copy of our recordings, trying to decipher my father's overture. I imagined Fitzgerald might have felt similarly when he set about to chronicle the Jazz Age, knowing it was

too soon to maintain a clear perspective. "The present writer already looks back to it with nostalgia," he wrote. After I left New York to attend college and travel, I assumed the obligatory gestures toward my father—sent postcards, telephoned on Christmas. During my visits home we met occasionally, for lunch in Manhattan, but our meetings were composed of disjointed conversation. In college I studied politics and literature, still searching for Dickensian virtue and rebellion, still idolizing Bob Kaufman, too. My father had assumed various new philosophies that seemed to profess a metaphysical detachment from the world. Though I tried to look back wistfully, I knew that years had solidified the fact that if he and I had ever been a band, we had long since split.

I listened to the CD that morning. The sound was crisp, clear. It picked up the interim noise that had blended into the vast background of the cassette recording: the start and stop of the tape recorder, the white noise between songs, even the muffled groan of traffic outside our apartment window. With each tune, the guitar's classical melody and my father's steady voice buttressed my wild young vocals. I hadn't mastered the microphone. The sound of my voice fluctuated from strident and piercing high notes to muted lows as if I had just begun to walk away. We may have given a mismatched performance, but we kept good time. We were bound in key.

I don't know why the package arrived when it did. Perhaps, just weeks before my college graduation—something of a milestone in my family—my father longed for old times. I couldn't be sure. After years of attempting to navigate the role of out-of-touch daughter, I didn't know my father at all. But listening to the recording, with the shrill of my own voice barreling through "Mary Had a Little Lamb" and the steady strum of his guitar in my ear, I realized: we shared a common history. Perhaps we might communicate, as we once had, through sound.

———

Paul McCartney has said that he wrote the song "Blackbird" about the struggle of African Americans during the civil rights movement shortly after the riots in Little Rock, Arkansas, when racial tensions in the state escalated in the spring of 1968. In an interview with Diane Sawyer, McCartney explained that he intended the blackbird to be a symbol of the black woman. McCartney couldn't have known how it felt to be a black woman in America in the 1960s any more than a black woman fighting for her rights in America would have known how it felt to be a Beatle. But when McCartney wrote "take these broken wings and learn to fly," it was a poetic appeal for strength over adversity. It is a song about perseverance, a song of support.

———————

My father's whole body moves when he laughs. After I ask him about the summer of 1970, his shoulders heave silently and he shakes his head as, I imagine, he pictures himself as a young man. I try to do the same—to see the lankiness of his adolescence, the dome of his hair, the thick glasses and thin mustache. Now when he smiles I notice the crow's-feet around his eyes, the new creases in his brow. My face is a facsimile of his. While the lines of my features are tweaked for more feminine angles, my cheeks still ball and blush like his, just as they did when I was a girl, when we laughed together and sang folk songs and rock 'n' roll.

We sat in a French café on West Fourth Street, at a wobbling table by a window. A voice recorder lay between us. I had decided to record my father. I was newly graduated and trying to be a journalist, but I was bitter and lost and needed to get my own stories straight. Our waiter approached and kneeled to wedge a piece of folded cardboard under the table's leg. My father, with two palms splayed flat on the marble surface, tested its balance, while I gripped a small vase filled with baby's breath and a synthetic red carnation. My father ordered a drink. I took a steady stream of coffee.

"Can that thing record with all the noise in here?" he asked.

Checking the recording light, I assured him everything was fine.

My father sipped his Scotch. He was dressed in a black turtleneck and slacks, like an aging Beat, a stoic panther. His hair, trimmed short, had begun to gray near his temples. "Where shall I start?" he asked.

I told him it didn't matter. I wanted to know everything.

"I made a few notes," he said, reaching into his jacket. He unfolded a piece of paper, put on his wire-rimmed glasses, and peered down at the page. He had made an outline. It was typed. I watched him trace his finger along an ash-colored line of the marble tabletop and look down into his plate. For as long as I can remember, my father has dropped his head when he recalls a feeling, the same as when he listens. After a moment he cleared his throat. His voice sounded strong, as if just tuned.

He began from the beginning.

That afternoon, during our first recording, my father told me about his earliest memories: of standing barefoot in a yard as he watched his family's house burn down in Western Pennsylvania; of the neighbor who gave him a secondhand violin and the miles he used to walk to reach his lessons in a nearby town. He told me about his first guitar, "the love of his life," about the day it was run over by a bus, and about how my mother saved up to buy him a new one, the one he still has to this day. He told me about the year he was drafted to Vietnam. Although his mother offered to send him to Canada, he reported as directed, to the Pittsburgh Induction Center, where he waited for hours before an officer, sizing him up, grew skeptical of his stance and deemed him unfit for service: flat feet. A month later, his friend Ronnie, a fellow tuba player and the life of the party, came home having lost both of his legs.

I may never know the most intimate details of my father's life or why, after years, he agreed without hesitation to let me record his story. Perhaps there is something that inspires us as adults to share who we are in the same way that as children we feel safely compelled to belt out our voices. Some of the best, most enduring songs in American music are reinvented. Nursery rhymes have lasted for centuries with new interpretations, new verses, and new hand gestures to serve succeeding generations. Perhaps in life and family, just as in music, we can only hope to rebuild, to relisten, to remix.

The remix is a sampling intended not to reconstruct but rather to repurpose. We are not rewriting history, just reimagining the tense and tempo of its verses, reassigning the beats—who gets beat, who holds the beat, who goes to war, who stays silent.

The thing about the boy in the Baptist church that has stayed with me was the way he sang with pure abandon. He had full lips that he licked and moistened in between lines, and the resonance of his voice emerging from such a small body carried an unexpected, chilling force.

"His Eye Is on the Sparrow" is not an easy song to sing, so when it is done right it's awe-inspiring. In the same way, I remember hearing Eva Cassidy's version of Pete Seeger's "Had I a Golden Thread" recorded shortly before her death in 1996. A world apart from Seeger's banjo folk song, Cassidy's version rang out as blues. Against a background of pounding funk and organ riffs, her vocals belt through each verse, transporting the lyrics in a hair-raising gospel of throaty high notes and crescendos that brought an old song back to life.

———————

Later that evening at home, after visiting with my father, I dug out a set of old headphones that fit snugly around my head and listened to the new recording. The intonation of his voice rose and fell with thoughtful reflection, and sometimes, with the excitement of a child, as he recalled memories of his youth, his teenage years, his wants and struggles into adulthood. When I reached the end of the recording, nearly three hours' worth of tape, I listened again. Each time I pulled new details from his voice, new meaning from the pool of sound, re-envisioning a man, filling the years of silence.

The sound of my own voice was surprisingly steady, near adult.

"Do you remember singing together?" I ask. This is the question that makes my voice crack, and spill into the ocean of sound between us. Awaiting his response all I really want to know is if he remembers the way I do, if he was present in our past. Between my question and his answer there is enough time to project the fate of this collaboration. This would be our B side, the second side of vinyl where record labels place, not the lesser tracks but the more experimental tunes, when the band lets loose and plays. But what if a short studio session in the fall of 1986 was all we had? What if our father-daughter duo wasn't the show-stopper I once believed it to be, but instead was nothing but hype?

But my father still repeats my questions with the same smiling tone he used when I was young: "Do I remember singing together?" When he speaks again it is both stern and gentle: "Those recordings . . ." His voice thins and retreats. I press the headphones against my ears, as if I might miss something. He is quiet for a long time. Then I hear the faint rumbling train of his breath—"You were really something," he says—and maybe we are bound for glory now.

A glass clinks against the tabletop; the café sounds its background noise. "You used to sing that one song over and over. I'd hear you singing to yourself, just under your breath . . ."

My father heightens his voice to imitate my straining falsetto.

"My . . . Fair . . . Lady . . ."

His deep laughter bathes the space around my ear. And in that moment, I wonder how he's kept his voice so strong. I wonder if maybe he's been out on the frontlines all this time—staying ahead of things until his name is next called so he won't be sent home, watching his friends return changed, watching his children grow up changed—keeping his fingers fast and nimble, the black knuckles of a jazzman dancing over the frets, his guitar tuned and burning, so he can keep the beat happening, can keep singing about blackbirds and sparrows all through the second side.

II

Daphne, Running

Still Life with Chair

A funny thing about a chair:
You hardly ever think it's there.

THEODORE ROETHKE

Lately, I've been going batty at the thought of stillness. Even sitting by a window feels like being in asylum. The world outside, cycling through its seasons, is complicit in our human associations. When it rains or snows, we remember: birthdays, anniversaries, memorials. When the leaves change and fall, we recollect: an early lesson in death, the night I first believed in love. It is harder, perhaps, to ground our perceptions in the consistency of common things: a bed, a desk, a chair.

———————————

I stood among the boys, who had clustered in a huddle of Oxfords and low-slung jeans, in a second-story room at a campus house party. Each with a whiskey glass and a streaming cigarette, they stood in staged rapture. Ben had waved me into the room as I passed in search of a free bathroom. "Come," he said. "We could use a feminine eye." So I joined them, gazing at a painting on the wall.

The canvas hung askew. Thickly coated in acrylic, the painting bore the abstract depiction of a chair, singular and empty, in a room of three distorted walls. I didn't recognize the painting, nor did I particularly care for it, but I appreciated the expressionist approach. The brush strokes echoed de Kooning; the bold primary colors resembled Newman or Mondrian—rich yellows, reds, an underpainting of blue. And it reminded me of the city I had recently abandoned for the Colorado mountains.

"The question is," Ben began, gripping his drink, "what is the nature of a chair?" He glanced at me from beneath the rim of his newsboy hat and scratched at the thin beard skirting his chin.

I've been trying to find order in the disorder of memory. I wonder what it means that I can't recall all of their names. Or have I tried to forget them? Most days their faces blend in a half-rendered backdrop, except for two ingrained and juxtaposed in the foreground of one night. The night we lost Ben; the night I found Joe. Sitting here, I can feel the seat of my chair hard beneath my body. The legs creak like dry branches or a slab of driftwood in the wind. I am alone with just an image becoming more and more singular, begging to be objectified like the myriad common things praised by Neruda's odes—*one chair, alone in the jungle.*

Chair: *a seat, with support for the back, designed to accommodate one person.* The word originates from the Greek *cathedra*, a compound of *kata* ("down") and *hedra* ("seat").

Early evidence of chairs dates to 2680 BC in ancient Egypt, where cave paintings, carvings, and hieroglyphics depicted seated figures. Across the Euphrates, stone funerary carvings on monuments revealed the existence of chairs in Mesopotamia. The most famous ancient chair was in fact a throne (from Indo-European origin meaning "to hold or support"). Tutankhamen's throne (circa 1333–1323 BC), built of wood and encased in gold, was excavated from the pharaoh's tomb in 1923.

"Consider," Ben continued. "Did someone just get up, or is someone about to sit down?" His grin widened. A friend of mine in the sophomore class, someone I knew from back home, had insisted I attend the party that night; there were people to meet. Ben was one of them. Hip-hop beats and flirtatious laughter rose from downstairs as the boys carried on their charade, assuming theatrical gestures and affected accents of bohemian art junkies.

One noted the use of color while inhaling a cigarette. Another— long, lanky—leaned in until his nose nearly touched the canvas. Foreground brush strokes filled the surface with the color of saffron and cornmeal. Red sliced through the frame like rouge to form the angles of a chair, and a pool of blue added depth to the composition. Even now I'm not sure why the painting inspired such parody. But the image has ingrained itself in my card catalog of visual history—one

I can't help but pull from, looking for reference while sitting by a window.

In 1888, Vincent van Gogh painted two of his well-known works while in the company of Paul Gauguin at Arles. *Vincent's Chair*, housed in London's National Gallery, vibrates with van Gogh's signature golds and blues and depicts a simple straw chair positioned on a wood slab floor. A crumpled handkerchief with tobacco and the artist's pipe rests in the seat. Conversely, *Gauguin's Armchair*, exhibited in Amsterdam's Rijksmuseum, is darkly ornate—a "somber reddish-brown wood," as van Gogh described it in a letter to critic G. Albert Aurer, "the seat of greenish straw," with a lighted torch and two strewn novels.

Plato's Theory of Forms uses the example of a chair to suggest that a material object is merely an imitation of its ideal form. The ideal form, in turn, constitutes the object's true reality. The essence of a chair is its "chairness."

Maybe it was a riddle after all. "A trick question," Ben said, his mouth curling at the taste of whiskey. I couldn't help but indulge him. "So, what is the nature of a chair?" He linked his arm in mine. "Wouldn't you agree that both are true? Someone stands, someone else sits down. Someone comes, someone goes." His voice carried the scent of bourbon; its cadence seesawed between playful and profound. The other boy, distracted by his own amusement, rubbed his eyeglasses against his shirt and placed them back on the bridge of his nose, to offer: "like a glass half empty or half full." I felt the wine I nursed in slow sips begin to flush and color my cheeks, and I chose not to prolong the discussion by noting that the *perspective* of a chair and the *nature* of a chair are, in fact, two different things. By then it hardly mattered. The boys broke character and began roughhousing over a bummed cigarette. The sight of them morphed into a tangle of limbs and choke holds.

The American painter Andrew Wyeth all but immortalized the Windsor writing chair when he placed the lone object in the center of a composition. Realistically rendered against the dark beige walls of a Pennsylvania bedroom, Wyeth's *Writing Chair*, painted in 1961, is empty except for a dark captain's jacket draped over one arm.

In Latin, the phrase *ex cathedra*, meaning "from the chair," was once commonly applied to the Pope's declarations on faith or morals as contained in divine revelation or, at least, intimately connected to something greater.

———

Why do we remember certain details? What is it about them that holds us? Before the window I assume the restive pace of a captive. Sitting again in this simple chair, imagining it otherwise—*a throne of unkempt velvet . . . the plush of an overstuffed chair*—perhaps I'll find the calm sensibility and decorum of a lady. Either way, I will stay here long enough to call upon the archival instinct to reconstruct and conserve the mundane pieces of a moment: The way I wrapped a cardigan close around my chest as I waited outside the house that night. How earlier that day the campus grounds flaunted a palette of autumn where rusty hues mingled with blond cottonwoods and golden beeches. Or the fact that just before I saw Joe coming toward me, as I gripped the porch railing, trying to seem at ease, I noticed the toe of my tennis shoe dotted with a fresh stain of red wine.

I'd first seen Joe on his bicycle weeks before while sitting one morning by the library. With one hand on his handlebars and a book clamped under his arm, he pedaled effortlessly. And because attraction really does defy dimension and morph everything it knows, as he passed, his cool glance spanned the length of the quad. And then, like every morning since, his eyes (brown, docile, animal) reached across the lawn to mine (green, dewy, smitten). So when he stood beside me with his hands in his pockets, toeing at a stone in the grass, it seemed an inevitable moment. We fumbled through introductions. I tried not to blush when I noticed the gap between his front teeth. My arms clasped my body in a straightjacket hold because it felt impossible to stand still. He asked if I was cold. Even now I remember the ache in the back of my legs and wonder how odd it is that we say "weak" in the knees, when it's so clearly the strength of the pulse running through the body.

In *One and Three Chairs*, 1965, Joseph Kosuth places a chair against a wall. To its left hangs a life-size photograph of that same chair. To its right, an enlarged photostat of the definition of the word *chair*.

The installation, on view at New York's Museum of Modern Art, asks viewers to consider how these three representations communicate the common fact of the object. We see a chair. We see the visual image of a chair. We see the etymological definition of a chair. How do they differ? Which representation constitutes the true nature of the form? Which has more chairness?

On Walden Pond, Henry David Thoreau furnished his ten-by-fifteen-foot cabin with a bed, a table, a writing desk, and three chairs: "one for solitude, two for friendship, three for society."

———

Given the chance, the more sober minded would probably have known better, or foreseen the danger that night. But autumn was around us, fallen in leaves of gold, and in its death we were alive and young in that back-to-school-special sort of way, all promise and adventure. When Ben reappeared bounding from the house, he slung an arm around Joe and, glancing between the two of us, seemed to slow down for a moment—to come back to earth again, just long enough to say, "So you found him."

The two of them jabbed elbows and laughed like schoolboys before Ben spun away singing a scat-style tune, waving and yelling alongside another guy that they'd meet us at the dorm. Their bodies held in shadow against the campus lights, the brim of Ben's newsboy hat outlined in a sharp yellow glow.

———

Years ago, riding the subway in Manhattan, I watched a man offer his seat to an elderly woman. She nodded politely. Once seated, she turned to recognize that the woman next to her was a childhood friend. The two women reunited, tearing up with disbelief. Then the woman stopped short and looked around. "Where's that sweet young man?" she kept saying. "Where'd he run off to?" I looked too, but he was gone.

———

Details are as relentless as they are invaluable. Memory is maddening. I want to stand and spin my chair like a prop in a musical. Sitting backward now, my thighs stretch wide to straddle the seat, my chest hugs the carved wooden rods of the straight back. Its curves and mine embrace, just for an instant. Then I am up again, swinging one leg over the side like Liza Minelli in *Cabaret*, because I cannot bear to sit still.

———

Later that night, as Joe and I walked east, away from the mountains, he explained the tradition of exploring the catacombs of campus—a grid of utility tunnels nestled below school grounds. I asked if it was dangerous. We bit our lips and laughed, and his laughter, somehow familiar, warmed the air around my cheeks. We continued across campus to meet the others, beneath the soaring contour of Pikes Peak stenciled against the indigo sky, above the underworld carved in the earth below, amid the dry leaves still whispering at our feet. In a way, I think part of us is buried in those whispers, the risk, the romance, the way we relished uncertainty and believed it could never harm us.

———

Presenting the chair as portrait, van Gogh may have intended his two paintings to evoke the artists' contrasting temperaments. In art books or on the occasion they are exhibited together, *Vincent's Chair* and *Gauguin's Armchair* often appear side by side, facing away from each other, as if to suggest a volatile relationship between the two men. But much depends on how you look at it. Facing one another, the paintings may speak to a mutual, although grudging respect.

———

In the fifth grade, a boy in my class kept rocking back and forth in his chair. After berating him repeatedly, our teacher dragged him to his feet. "If you can't sit still, then you'll have to stand," she said, determined to make an example of him. He stood, fidgety and shamed. I looked across the room and exchanged a conspiring glance with my friends. And as if by instinct—some act of fair-dealing bravado—we stood, wailing: "If he has to stand, then we won't sit." In minutes our loyal classmates followed suit. The scrape of wooden chairs on linoleum echoed through the room. In our small-scale triumph, it seemed as if the world had opened before us.

———

When we reached the dorm, it was nearly midnight. People filtered in and out of the confines of someone's dorm room. I sat on the edge of a crowded couch and watched a couple dancing nearby: the boy's rutted brow, the girl's puckered lips, hips swaying in abstract circles, arms slicing through the air. I caught Joe's stare across the room. The crowd around us began to thin, and I could see a faint movement in his shoulders. My hands grew clammy; my cheeks reddened as if I had stumbled upon the throne of lust and longing and was given a moment to sit—in *a chair that embraces everything, the sound ground and supreme dignity of repose*—before time continued, and I smiled. I remember the precise moment I smiled, too, as if it marked the moment of my concession, the surge of instinct when something inside me decided I would like this one above the rest.

––––––––

In the second grade, I suffered a crush on a boy from my class who, one day, pulled a chair out from under me just as I bent to sit down. My bony ass, and then my hard stubborn head, slammed against the floor. The room erupted in laughter. I nursed bruises for weeks. The next day he told me that I had pretty hair, and then he said, "Sometimes it hurts when we like things so much."

––––––––

Now I am standing again. Nose to windowpane, breath whiting out the leaves outside, I'm thinking about how easily things grow hazy and obscured. Death carries its own dimension. Shock inevitably fogs the view. If I stood on this chair, circling the seat on tiptoes, and tried to peer into meaning or tried to unearth the epicenter of narrative, I would find little but a balancing act, wobbly legs and all.

––––––––

I still wonder how we knew where to look that night, how we determined that something was wrong. I remember a shift in the nearby voices, which dislodged me from my reverie in the possibility of Joe, to recognize that most everyone had been ushered out of the room until just a few of us remained. Someone was pacing, saying, "They should have been here by now. It's been hours." We stood clustered in the center of the room silently, drunkenly, courting worst-case scenarios, until someone broke trance and volunteered to stay behind, "in case they show," while the rest of us pivoted toward the door.

––––––––

Beginning in 1963, Andy Warhol revealed his darkest work to date with a series of screen prints called *Electric Chairs*. This series, housed in several museums including the Tate and the Walker Art Center, is part of his larger *Death and Disaster* period and offers a then rare glimpse into an execution chamber. In one purple-tinged print and another bathed in red, the word *Silence* appears in the top right corner of the room. The image evokes those that have sat there before and those who may follow. Yet it is neither condemnation nor celebration. Warhol, who often refused to discuss his work beyond elusive statements such as "There's nothing behind it" or "I like boring things," simply provides a representation. Interpretation lies at the mercy of the viewer.

———

It is difficult to find in language a worthy match for the euphoria of being young and high and falling in love. So much depends on the quickening pace of everything: breath, the air, everything propelling forward so there is little choice but to follow in oblivion. I remember how fast our feet moved as we looked for our friend that night. I could hear one boy's breath heaving as, two paces ahead, he led us across the lawn and through the vacant parking lot that lay bathed in the vermilion glow of the campus security posts. Another boy trailed after him, trying to reason while keeping stride—"They must have lost track of time. What could have possibly gone wrong?" We continued, an anonymous crew of boys and girls parading toward a darkness we sensed but didn't know. I heard Joe's footsteps behind me. As we hurried, he took my hand and linked his arm in mine. I can still recall how his forearm pulsed against my own—so much life surging beneath our skin—and the sick happiness I felt amid the strangeness of running as we did toward red flashes wavering across campus.

As our breath shortened, the air felt peculiar. I could hear our feet heavy on the ground, the wind whistling around us. As we neared the library, the crimson lights of an ambulance churned through the dark like a flaming carousel but quiet—no doors slamming shut, no engine idling at the ready to rush toward help—just stillness. Red light. Silence.

———

Odd to think that a chair, an invention of such simplicity, is an artifact that we have come to take for granted. We see and touch chairs not with our eyes and hands alone but with our entire bodies. When we are tired, we sit. When we dine, we sit. When we read, when we write, when we confess our sins and ask forgiveness. The simple presence of a chair, like the unbridled promise of life when we are young, is a common assumption: we trust that the structure will hold us. But what if a chair is pulled aside, what if it breaks suddenly beneath you?

As I picked myself up, the sound of my chair against the floor must have startled the starlings outside. Back in my seat, I am trying to remain here, one leg curled beneath me like a girl, so I'm not so tempted to tip forward again to catch a better view. The breath on the windowpane has cleared and the details glow anew. I can see the lines of the leaves again, the composition of the branches, just before the sky turns—Bring me a chair in the midst of thunder.

——————

Death by electrocution can be, but is not always, instantaneous. When Ben removed a manhole cover just north of the library and descended, not into the tunnels as intended, but into an unmarked electrical vault, did he know he had stepped into an accident? His feet were firmly grounded when his hand touched a live wire, and I wonder if he felt the eight-thousand-volt current through his body. Did he think of his parents, his first love, of sex or lightbulbs, of leaves and lightning, of the Rosenbergs, of Warhol? Or was there nothing at all but for the surge and the Silence?

——————

Even the most common artifacts support multiple representations. Each of Thoreau's three chairs served a different purpose. Warhol's chair mainly served one. Kosuth's three chairs, seemingly different, are one and the same; they question the notion of representation itself. According to Roethke, "to know a Chair is really it, you sometimes have to go and sit." Ben's definition of the chair in the painting that night was aptly ephemeral, embodying a transient duality of arrival and departure, past and future. Someone comes, someone goes. Death, yet life.

——————

Am I trying with this recollection to compose a scene or paint a picture? One seems dependent on movement, the other on stillness. The racing adrenaline of tragic accident. The numbness of loss. The view from a window arouses and fragments the narrative of memory into images that resurface like a dream: The morning after, the sky carried the faint residue of siren light. Joe lay beside me, his breath steaming and cooling the back of my neck. I inhaled the smell of his hands: the balmy trace of soap and cigarettes, the steely salt he had wiped from my eyes. I felt for the small beating just inside his wrist—*here*, *still*.

———

During the Eighth International Istanbul Biennial in 2003, Colombian sculptor Doris Salcedo filled a gap between two buildings in the city's ironmonger district with sixteen hundred wooden chairs. Communicating both chaos and absence, what surreal moment might one discover—what twist of fate to stumble across a once-familiar alley filled with a four-story mass grave of chairs? How do they balance, caught in a still cascade? How do we make sense of such incongruous logic?

———

Sometimes I think the world is a crowded waiting room that we fill, sitting and standing, pacing and leaning, waiting for our name to be called, afraid of the crisp white coats and of the cool touch of a stethoscope against our skin, which will tell us just how alive we really are.

In just two days we would attempt to celebrate Joe's birthday, and a week later, my own. When the arrangements were complete for a memorial on campus, we would plant a tree in Ben's memory because that is what people often do. Each year the tree's leaves change from pale to deep green to yellow and gold, and when the light shifts, as it shifts now, the saw-toothed leaves shimmy on their branches like gilded chandeliers, before dropping to the ground to spin beneath the feet of lovers and dreamers and freshmen and seniors, just trying to learn something, to outlive the years we all deserve.

———

And what if I were in some ballroom lit with gold chandeliers—or for that matter, an old gymnasium full of streamers and strobe lights, and walls lined with bleachers and color-schemed balloons—waiting for a boy to sweep me onto the floor? Forget about the electric chair, all that energy surging through a body, and raise a chair to dance the hora, or swing one overhead, tap its narrow legs against the concrete courts like the step dancers back home practicing for the homecoming show. Or a wrestler, flailing a chair into the ring, challenging the world to a brawl.

Hans Hofmann, an abstract expressionist painter, once said that "the whole world, as we experience it visually, comes to us through the mystic realm of color." That night Ben and I and the other boys had talked about the abstract image of a chair, analyzing the brush strokes, mocking the philosophical nature of it all. I woke the next morning to an aching realization. I wished I could have shared then what I know now—that the nature of a chair exists in how we view it. And that if I had three chairs I would paint them the three primary colors from which all others can be formed: red for death, yellow for life, blue for love. I would have told Ben this before he dashed off through the fallen leaves, leaving the rest of us strolling in a bath of moonlight.

———

Maybe I don't have to assume the lens of a patient or prisoner, but there is a certain confinement to sitting by a window, a sense of internment reserved for the elderly, the housebound, or melodramatic children pining away for snow, something laced with longing, even a little boredom —just a chair by the window: straight back, timber legs, and the body. How could I not move restlessly, spinning and squatting like a burlesque dancer contorting over a chair? Its inanimate thing-ness, its quotidian inertia, instills an endless signaling to the brain—*a single chair is the first sign of peace*: remember, believe, grow unabashedly nostalgic, see in color, feel in motion, dance a little more.

Babel, Notes on Tourism

Language has built towers and bridges,
but itself is inevitably as fluid as always.
HART CRANE

In March 2005, I stood among a crowd in La Plaza Nueva, twenty-two, far from home, wondering where girlhood had gone and thinking how, if language were a party, a dinner table set for four or five with cocktails and caviar—we would have crashed its intentions long ago, invited ourselves and our closest friends to attend, knocking down flutes of champagne as we brushed through the door, and would have woken the next morning not remembering a thing. Because there is nothing more decadent or sacred, nothing more delicate or savage than to scrounge for meaning in our varied lexicon—the dialects we are born with, and those we never know.

At noon, the Seville center fell silent as people bowed their heads to honor the dead. Diego stood beside me. His hands shuffled in his pockets and through his hair. March 11 marked the anniversary of the Madrid train bombings nearly six hundred kilometers north of Seville, when a cacophony of explosions erupted on commuter trains during a Thursday morning rush hour. Nearly two hundred dead, hundreds more wounded.

As the sun rose above the plaza, roosters echoed from obscured posts on rooftop patios—the high-risen backyards of children, adorned with sun chairs and clotheslines—now otherwise quiet. A woman with creased skin and wounded eyes, carrying sagebrush, handed me two candles. I passed one to Diego to steady his hands. The smell of beeswax reminded me of home, of making candles with my mother as a girl. The woman whispered in Spanish. "It's been a year," she said. "But it seems like only yesterday." She smelled of fresh bread and garlic, as she lit my candle's virgin wick with her own, turned, and lowered her head in prayer.

I listened as the movement of her lips suggested sorrow—wishing I could hear the words she recited. Thinking how every time I hear the soft whisper or thick groan of an accent I want to find its roots. I want to trace the years of its migration, to follow the sound like a strand of Ariadne's yarn leading through the labyrinth to a center where words, still damp with amniotic dew, first inhabited breath.

———

A week earlier, I had sat waiting for Diego in the café across from the community center where he taught English—the same center where I had studied Spanish during the first week of my stay. The crowd shifted, shouting orders of coffee and *bocadillos*. The shop owner paced behind the bar setting saucers, clearing teaspoons like a one-man xylophone act, china clinking against the marble countertop. Smoke rose and hovered in a faint haze above the bar. A couple nuzzled in a corner by the window. The man paused his banter to nibble at the woman's ear as she exhaled laughter with the smoke of her cigarette.

I had been in Spain nearly three weeks, having temporarily deserted college and left behind the boy I loved. This, according to my mother, meant "my feet were cold," but really I just needed space. Back in the States, though I had moved to Colorado and hadn't been home to New York City in months, I knew nine-to-fivers still artfully avoided the lower Manhattan canyon where the Twin Towers once stood, which now has been filled in and stretches back toward the sky, but at the time felt fossilized like a chipped tooth or a chicken pox scar, which many of us have but all remember differently.

In Seville, my terraced flat lay among the clay-shingled rooftops of the Barrio de Santa Cruz. Once the city's Jewish quarter after the thirteenth-century Christian conquests, Santa Cruz is a tangle of narrow alleys, cobblestoned squares, and ancient gardens. Galleries, guesthouses, and chic cafés are mere notions of modernity against the cerulean-tiled mosques, ornate cathedrals, and frescoed palaces—each bearing testimony to its own chapter in a once-harmonious religious past.

They say that as long as Seville has straddled the Guadalquivir River, the orange trees have held their juice. Like for most cities, its history is embedded in the skeletal framework of modern civilization—from which we extract language like marrow from bone, to make meaning, to build towers and cathedrals and palaces of memory.

I envy the way buildings, like certain bodies, bear distinct marks of their architectural identity. Unlike the in-between ambiguity that colors my skin, my hair, my voice: a little Manhattan where I was born, a little "outer borough" where I was raised, the slow laze I picked up when I was in love in the Pacific Northwest, the subtle brogue I stumbled upon in Ireland, the way I learned to use my tongue in Spain. Is the anonymity of speech an extraction of cultural identity? Is this my grandfather's concept of "cosmopolitan" elegance? He, the man who fled a suburban middle-class life to run with the horses and study reservations out west, the man who took years to accept the way my parents' marriage blended the border between black and white, the way they brought two children into the world, the way they named them.

At the end of the counter, two men in polished suits stood over a splayed newspaper, gesturing with twin cigars, their voices mere rumblings in the crowd. I glanced at my watch. Time in Spain is a loose abstraction. Still, Diego was usually punctual.

He was only a boy when Franco died. But Spanish history, every date and detail, ran through Diego like a bloodline. His father, who had recently passed, had left testament to Spain's civil war and the years of state repression that followed. To Diego he had bequeathed his stories—of book burnings and disappearances, of mass graves throughout the country. "Es muy complicado," Diego would say, pausing as he explained the "pact of silence" that had enveloped the country in an erasure of collective memory.

Finally, I saw him. He removed his thick-rimmed glasses as he entered the café and made his way toward me. I could see his odd expression, his crumpled brow.

"What is it?" I asked. "Un café?" I turned to my cup, pinching at the porcelain handle.

"Someone asked for you at the center," Diego said, leaning in close. "La policía."

The coffee singed my tongue. "The police?" I thought for a moment. "What could they possibly want with me?"

"I don't know," Diego shrugged. "They asked for you, by name. They wouldn't tell me anything more."

In my head, I inventoried the past few days for clues to what I might have done wrong. An assumed reflex, a defense I picked up growing up in the city, staying out too late in high school, trying to cover any number of offences—getting my story straight for my parents, my teachers. Which is not to say I was in any trouble with the law, but that as a young person testing out the extremes of the body, alive in the world, it's easy to lose track of even the minor misbehaviors.

Diego paid my bill. I slid off my chair, neglecting my bag, which tumbled awkwardly from my lap into Diego's hands. He placed it carefully on my shoulder.

"What do you think this is about?" I asked again.

Diego threw up his hands, "I don't know. *Vamos . . .*"

If this were the night of a party—that allegorical party I mentioned earlier—this would be the anticipatory walk to the door, wondering what the evening would bring, if I would be welcomed inside, offered a drink, wondering if I had worn the right shoes, or what beautiful stranger might be mingling nearby, ready to catch eyes across a room.

Inside the community center, a broad-shouldered officer stood waiting, a manila folder clamped under his arm. His uniform was crisp, his hair silver as he tipped his cap. He spoke slowly, long enough to establish that my Spanish was fully conversational; then he seemed to relax. Still, when he extended the courtesy of a third person in the room, another native speaker, "to be sure I understood," I accepted.

"Not you," the officer raised a hand to Diego, who stopped short. I wondered what he assumed about our relationship, if we had somehow insinuated conspiracy.

Diego was, indisputably, handsome. He resembled Goya's portrait of matador Pedro Romano. His dark hair fell in waves down to his cheekbones. His stoic expression broke eventfully when he laughed. In a short time we had forged an alliance of scholarly pursuit and an uninhibited love of dancing, awkward as we were.

But we each had our own preoccupations. Diego had lost his fiancée in a car accident just a year earlier. A detail he revealed to me one night, drunk from sherry, as we circled the Giralda Cathedral until dawn. He never mentioned it again. I offered little of my own crisis of commitment, as the boy I loved waited back in the States, and I half-wondered if he would still be there when I got home.

I remember telling Diego—perhaps that same night with the sherry and the cathedral—that one of the first words I learned in Spanish was the verb *amar*: to love. I may have tried to make meaning from this, see it as some preconceived lesson plan on the human condition, but it was little more than a loosely alphabetized eighth-grade vocabulary list. I remember, even now, how the word *amar* came just before *amenazar*, to threaten, and just after *alzar*, to lift, revolt, or rise above. On top of that, I was in the habit of watching Spanish soap operas late at night on Univisión, which is one a handful of channels we got growing up—and one of the few habits I have kept to this day. There is no greater indulgence in love and threats and convoluted plot lines than the *telenovela*.

Facing the officer's hand, Diego lost confidence. His expression dissolved into a childish pout. My palms grew clammy, my breath unsteady.

"Rosa?" I said to Diego.

Rosa, a plump administrative matriarch, oversaw the community center with a nose in everything within a two-mile radius of La Plaza Nueva. I had befriended her instantly when I arrived in Seville, and she'd helped me find a cheap rental in a nearby flat. She often questioned why I traveled alone and, at such a "ripe" age, was not married—and regularly consulted God on such matters as if he were present in the room. This was a small price for telephone access and a steady tap into the local gossip—which shop owners were the biggest "swingers," who met whom by the cathedral courtyard after hours—all unlikely dramatized scenarios adorned by Rosa's gift for gab.

"Miss, please . . ." the officer extended a long heavy arm toward me while issuing a side-glance at Diego, who ran off to fetch Rosa. I felt the puzzled gaze of a few bystanders as the officer led me down the hall into a classroom. The open windows had left a chill in the room. I felt distinctly foreign, alone—the pulse in my chest soothed only by the balmy smell of orange trees and pipe tobacco wafting from the courtyard.

"You know, from the sound of your name, I expected, well . . . un *hombre*, no?" he said pulling out a chair and motioning me to sit. "But no." He glanced down at me and his face softened as he spoke my name again, slowly. The sound clung to his throat then rolled easily off his tongue.

"Jericho. This is the name of a city, no?" he asked. "In Israel," he said before I could muster a response. "Are you Jewish?"

I shook my head.

"What is your religion?"

I offered am ambivalent shrug, hoping to dodge further questioning about religious affiliation or the origin of my name, which was an inevitable conversation starter. But my bohemian parents' 1970s art school romance, when they took to Eastern and Western religious texts to find "far out" references for their paintings, and later their children, didn't strike me as a story that would translate. Or maybe it would.

"Your parents then—they were the hippies?" the officer asked, his eyebrows cocked, a smirk dabbed the corners of his mouth.

I might have wondered how he deduced this so quickly, but it wasn't the first time since arriving in Spain that I had heard reference to the hippies with an off-centered trace of intrigue, even reverence, as if they were some iconic rock 'n' roll band. This, I speculated, had something to do with the kindred parallel between the American counterculture of the 1960s and '70s and the explosive cultural freedom that marked the dawn of Spain's post-Franco era. I estimated the officer to be more or less of this generation. And I'm not sure why, but something about that gave me hope, as if we might get along better, as if—whatever this revealed itself to be—we might get through it somehow, together.

I was named after a city with improbably high walls, which, like most great walls, like the strongest borders, the tallest towers and richest empires, fell at the will of a people. Joshua led the Israelites to the city, and all they had to do was circle its boundaries and shout, their united cry bringing down the barriers. Maybe that is a lesson more in voice than in language, but I've come to think of these things as close cousins in the battles of survival, the one enabling the other, the other giving meaning to the one.

"Excuse me, sir, what is this about?" I asked, unsure from where I had mustered the bravado to question him for an explanation—and yet, this couldn't possibly be about my name. My voice quivered through the words.

"I did wonder," he went on, ignoring my question. "The handwriting was so elegant."

"Sir . . ." I shifted in my chair. Though I had paused for an instant to consider my penmanship—years of obsessive-compulsive practice since we learned cursive writing in the third grade, copying word after word in my notebooks, rewriting sentences, entire paragraphs, until they looked just right—I tried to stay focused. I resented the distraction, the officer's finesse. I realize, now, that he was likely biding time until Rosa arrived. Rosa: my witness—which is to say *onlooker*, or *observer*, someone who sees.

Finally she materialized breathless at the door. Her dust-colored hair billowed at her neck, having slunk out of the tortoiseshell comb that secured the coil perched atop her head. She huffed over to a seat next to mine, lowered herself, and tapped my knee. Smoothing the creases of her apron dress, she settled with her hands folded in her lap.

The officer began. "Are you familiar with this?" He placed a small notebook in the center of the table. I recognized it instantly—the spiral binding and faded blue cover—as my own. I hadn't realized it was gone, but was relieved to see that everything seemed more or less in order—various loose-leaf notes remained neatly folded, tucked into the pages among postcards I had yet to send home, a pressed stem of sage an elderly woman had given me after foretelling my future. I saw the edge of an old photograph I kept nestled in the back cover, the boy from back home and me stopped on the side of a road somewhere in Montana, smiling into the camera during the summer we drove from Seattle to New York.

"This was recently found at *El Corte Inglés*," the officer said.

The previous day's grocery shopping appeared like a slide show: the woman at the checkout line fidgeting with her brightly flowered head scarf, eyeing me as I calculated enough Euros to pay and finagled an armful of groceries; the couple behind me briskly pawing, like all couples in Spain who seemed just minutes away from making love; my notebook left forgotten on the counter.

I fielded the officer's questions. *Where was I born? Why was I in Spain? Are you aware of the terrorist factions that operate in this country?*

"Ay . . ." Rosa glanced up at the ceiling and crossed her chest.

My body stiffened around the pounding—as if miles of steel and concrete were falling—in the center of my chest.

"You have extensive notes here," he said and flipped to an earmarked page where annotations from my immersion class appeared in ballpoint ink.

Suddenly I understood.

He read aloud. It was from the day we discussed "*las noticias*"—bombings in the capital, September 11, *el 11 de marzo*, the Leganés Siege, the plots and politics of ETA, names, dates, landmarks. This, I remember, gave me some relief—just class notes, after all—easy to explain. But then the sound of the words, first in English and then the Spanish translations, contorted and sliced through the air as the officer glanced from my eyes down to the page: *los bombardeos, los secuestros, atentado terrorista, atentado suicida, la guerra santa.*

All at once, the room was buzzing with the sound of the words, which filled the space like careless teenagers, gossiping socialites, reveling and extravagant boozers, none of whom belonged.

The officer paused his recitation and asked if I had anything to say.

But where to begin? One could certainly explain the contents of my notebook—terms and expressions that had against my will taken on the essence of brutality. Read aloud, what I had hoped was accurate reportage played back as violent vocabulary, a recipe, a blueprint, a wish list. It was all wrong.

"You must understand," the officer began again, placing his hands flat on the table as if to steady himself. "In these times we must take precautions against any and all potential threats."

I wanted to tell him that I understood—I understood Spain's long-standing history of violence. This is what I had come to learn about, what Diego had taught me—about the past thirty years, about the various manifestations of the Basque militant ETA, of the assassinations in the 1980s, and yes, of the March 11 bombings in Madrid that added yet another point of conflict to a country long unable to agree on much of its history. "It's all very complicated." This, I understood. But the words knotted and collapsed in my throat. My stammers piled up like debris between us.

"Señor," Rosa began. "There must be some misunderstanding—"

I sat numb, except to Rosa's glare, and then composed myself enough to chime over her and assure the officer that my notebook was not a blueprint for terrorism but simply a journal. I was in his country as little more than a rogue romantic, a journalism student gone AWOL. I had nothing but admiration for Spain. I thought I might live there one day.

A burning blush filled my cheeks and I knew my frustration had by now settled into a stubborn contortion of features, the same sulking grimace I bore as a girl when I knew I was misunderstood, when I couldn't conjure the right words.

"Please, speak candidly," he said, perhaps, sensing my unease.

Maybe it was the professorial tone in his voice—the refined dinner host controlling his table, making his guests comfortable despite their awkward party fouls and blunders—that I registered as an opening. My nervousness dismantled into indignation. I found myself, without forethought or restraint, embarking on a minor rant, debunking the flawed politics of the "war on terror." How remembering my father stuck in the subway tunnels beneath Wall Street while others jumped from buildings above, through the pink dust, through the scent that would linger in the air, still didn't explain why our neighbor who owned Mike's Candy Store on the corner disappeared, was detained for months because his real name was Mohammed, because his wife wore a veil. Which led me more or less to the present absurdity regarding my notebook, which was by then an obvious mistake and an unfortunate waste of the officer's time.

"It's ridiculous—I mean, don't you think it's ridiculous?" I felt a pinch on my thigh and Rosa's eyes again.

"Ay, Dios . . . Señor, she doesn't know what she says," Rosa pleaded.

The officer raised a hand. Rosa slumped into silence, biting her lip.

"I'm sorry," I said.

And I was sorry. It had been a spotty monologue at best, and he was not the appropriate audience. He seemed a kind man and, I suspected, a fine officer—no more deserving of misdirected anxieties than I claimed to be. I felt the sting of my own hypocrisy. Worse yet, I could only imagine the officer's disappointment that he had spent the afternoon in pursuit not of a threat to national security but merely another heart-bleeding, entitled American.

But again, I couldn't find the words. The truth was that I didn't know how to describe my admiration, or what I perceived as the humbling effects of Spain. I didn't know how to explain the asymmetry between the popular response of Spanish citizens to their government and what I had seen back home in the States. That in a way, the events of the previous year marked not a blind rallying point, but an affirmation of the nation's democracy. Three days after the bombings in Madrid, the Spanish people voted to repudiate the Popular Party government's erroneous accusations as to who had been responsible for the attacks and elected the Spanish Socialist Workers' Party to lead the country. I had longed to witness this type of citizen reform in the States: "people power" that, like a suspension bridge, could transform our collective human narrative into a poetry of action.

"*Señor, por favor.* Will you have to take her away?" Rosa was fanning herself.

He studied my face then looked down. For a moment he became lost in the grain of the tabletop. On the surface, the afternoon light tossed arabesque shadows through the iron shutters in the window and spilled onto the floor set with richly glazed Moroccan tiles. It was the hour when teenagers sauntered through the streets. The Giralda Cathedral would be brimming with tourists as the shops and cafés closed up for an hour or two. The children would be out soon, peeling off their Catholic school uniforms. I wanted to grab my notebook—even just the photograph barely peeking out of the page with the top corner of Montana sky—and join them, running alongside the children, shedding off years in the sun.

The officer sat silently, paging through my notebook. I watched his lips move faintly over the words. I wondered how much he had read, to what extent he knew my manic insecurities, my stubborn sense of autonomy and desire for commitment. I wondered, too, if this would be the strip search that might expose my greatest fears, a failure to be young and in love, the deep cavities I kept crammed like a piece of baggage in my chest. Suddenly I felt naked before this man, who looked dignified in blue and whose hands, though rough-knuckled, I imagined to be smooth. I wanted to meet him in the café across the street and share a cigarette while we laughed about "that time" he questioned me in an empty schoolroom. I wanted to know what he

thought, what he felt. Did he have a wife at home? A mistress somewhere? I wondered how my name must have looked to him, strange,
foreign, the way it has always looked to me except on the rare occasion
when it has been made beautiful: when the boy back at home would
escape our bed at midnight, the deep rattle of paint cans in his pack, to
bomb boxcars by the highway, bridges along the river. *Bomb*: which is
to say *tag*, which is to say *paint* quickly, with subversive grace or a spy's
anonymity. I wonder who might have seen the letters of my name
passing throughout the western states like urban love letters, smitten
telegraphs from old-school b-boys throughout the alleys and tunnels
of the city. Sometimes he'd paint all seven letters of my name, as if
each were composed on a separate day of the week, sometimes my initials, a nickname, blocked out in six-foot letters beneath a bridge, that
stayed up for weeks before the city painted over it and only a black box
remained where my name once was, and every time I walked across
that bridge there was a little emptiness, the echo of frantic joy—

Did he know that feeling? Had anyone ever broken his heart? I
wanted to ask the officer, but I held my tongue as I noticed Rosa stealing a glance at her wristwatch.

"Señor?" she said regaining his attention, her concern now laced
with impatience.

"There's no need," the officer said with a certain geniality I had to
assume was more for Rosa's sake than my own exoneration. "Minor
paperwork should put the whole thing to rest."

The officer rose. "This, I believe, belongs to you," he said, handing
over my notebook. "You may want to keep a better eye on it. An old
lady caused quite a scene at *El Corte Inglés* when she found it."

I looked at Rosa. She stood quickly, thanked the officer, and with a
hard pat on my cheek, left to tend to her busy work.

In the main hall, the officer made a photocopy of my passport. Over
the buzz of the Xerox machine I heard old men milling about the
patio, their lazy talk and throaty laughter stirring the orange trees.

"So, the young man in the photo," the officer looked over at me
without turning his head, "where is he?"

"Back home."

"And the young man who brought you here—the one who wanted
to remain with you?"

"A friend," I said.

I felt he wanted a more distinct word to apply here. But what can words do? I could be a terrorist, a tourist, a tortured witness of human lore. I could track twisters on the plains or turn tricks in foreign cities. I could travel to La Grotte Chauvet and stare into the markings without ever knowing that the image of a horse's running legs means "love" in an endangered language or "home" in a dialect now extinct. How often do words hold us hostage, tortured in the unjust war of trying to understand the world? The world: which is to say, *each other*—which is to say, *everything*. I would rather lean into the body of misunderstanding than be nailed down by language, held captive by labels. I would rather lurk within the labyrinth of bewilderment, stumbling in circles as if under a spell, woozy and swaying between indulgence and intimacy—my staying power for the one, my flight risk for the other. *Amenazar*: to threaten. *Amar*: to love.

Thankfully, the officer did not pry further. He simply tipped his hat—all gentleman, no judgment—and, with a wink toward my notebook, handed me my passport and said something about "him" being a "lucky boy."

The Xerox machine issued a final sputter. I watched my face emerge upside down, get stuck halfway, and then shoot out into the paper tray, the U.S. watermark an opaque highlight over my grainy forehead. And then I was gone, tucked in a folder, filed away in a dusty cabinet of inconsequence, bedding down with countless carbon-copy testimonies and blank reports—all of us characters in untold tales and insignificant leads.

Before then, I had been a peripheral citizen in a small borderless world with endless stories reaching toward the sky, swabbing heaven for fingerprints to see which ones might be a match. An ancillary character in the handmade chapbooks of boys and men: Book of Jacob, Joseph, Daniel, John, narratives of confounded tongues. And though the canon is incomplete, I wonder if it matters that I never really understood the things they said. So many words are lost to exquisite affairs, so many metaphors and similes get buried beneath the sentimental language of love. Before then, I had been the objective narrator in the chapters and testaments of identity—those of my parents and the racial boundaries they struggled to overcome; those of my Muslim neighbors forced to account for their livelihood. Now, I picture the file cabinet where my name resides in a stiff metal drawer like the chambers of a city morgue. I imagine my file, in the absence of my body, lying down on the cold metal platform beside men and women with odd names from odd cities, that no one can identify, that no one has come to claim.

———

The following week, I stood in the plaza. An occasional breeze flickered the candle flames and filled the air with the scent of beeswax and citrus, smoke and sage. I leaned toward Diego and lit the wick of his candle with my own. In another week, I would travel toward the southern coast, to the city of Cádiz. Diego embodied what I had come to understand as the great paradox of Spain, a country with an unparalleled instinct for pleasure and festivity and the innate understanding of loss. It was hard to imagine continuing on without him.

Maybe, instead of being named for a city known for its walls, I should have been named after Babel—another ancient town with an infamous tower, from the Hebrew *balal*, meaning to jumble, or *lebalbel*, to confuse. The place where brick was forged for stone and a tower built, where once earth was of one language, until those same words were irrevocably scattered. Where language became so confounded that the city, intended to unify humanity, was left as an abandoned thought. Babel— unconventional to be sure, as far as names go, even for my parents, the hippies that they were. But is there any narrative that better explains the phenomenon of language, the multiplicity of meaning, human existence, or desire?

I wonder how much of our disorder lies not in the limitations of what we see, hear, touch, taste, and smell, but in the mishandling of words: what we speak but do not mean; what we write but cannot say. What is the difference between a traveler and a tourist? Between a native and a local, to be of a place, not merely from it? To ensure safety, to protect security, which to some might mean to *engage*—which is to say, *wage impossible war.*

At the far end of the square, a group of uniformed officers of the Guardia Civil stood clustered. I recognized the silver hair of my officer among them. He seemed uncomfortable in the heat. I watched him adjust his collar and noticed, for the first time, the decorations on his uniform.

As the cathedral bells resonated throughout the city, hundreds of people stood in prayer. Again, my eyes found the officer. A week earlier I had been in an empty classroom, fielding his questions as he determined whether I was a threat to his country. Now we filled the same space of mourning, the same body of loss. He looked foggy and distant, like one of those faces that inevitably looks familiar in the morning when you wake up remembering little of the night before, except how at one point the pace of the music changed and how you may have shared a slow dance with a stranger—yes, the way you let your head rest on his shoulder, the way his voice whispered your name—and how odd that was, and how perfectly sad. The officer glanced up and for an instant I caught his eye squinting into the sun before I looked away. Later, I wondered if he saw me, one face in a crowd, lips moving in my own silent prayer: *amenazar, amar, alzar*—*to threaten, to love, to rise above.*

Of Things Lost

Sardina pilchardus

LAGOS, PORTUGAL

The balmy smell of fish wafted through the air before the waiter reached my table. He set down a bread basket and a plate of grilled sardines. "For the lady," he said and winked. When I arrived to dine alone, the same young man had fumbled the silverware as he cleared the extra place setting and slid a small vase of wildflowers into the void.

A television, set in the corner by the ceiling, broadcast updates on a missing girl from England. She was barely five years old. Outside, the humble exterior of *A Igreja de Santo António* stood tall.

On my plate, the sardines lay in trinity, their eyes like black onyx, their bodies still, radiant, silver. Silver like the subway cars back home. Silver like the antique hand mirror passed down from Grandmother to Mother and then to me. And though I haven't yet mothered my own, I will pass it on again, one day.

My mother is a fish, I think. The words sound as litany in my head. That same trip, in a Lisbon bookshop, I found Faulkner and his infamous five words. *My mother is a fish.* It's her hair, I think. It must be her hair. Once a blonde flower-laced bob, my mother's hair is silvery gray now against the marine blue of her eyes.

By the tail end, I plucked a sardine from my plate, placed it atop a wedge of bread, and peeled back the crisp layer of skin. Scales fell from my fingers like flakes of muscovite.

Sardines are the fish of Saint Anthony—Anthony of Padua—who, I learned, was not Italian but Portuguese. He was also a seaman. While visiting the Adriatic coast, he preached to the fish. Large fish and fingerlings lined up at the shore, heads buoyed in the water, gills ajar, bowing in reverence. The townspeople, hearing the commotion, ran to witness the miracle at sea. And now, the opening of the local fishing season coincides with the Feast of Saint Anthony in June. Patron of sailors, of ocean voyages and safe travel, Saint Anthony is most invoked for the recovery of things lost.

I remember a sign for the missing girl on the window by my table. In the Algarve, home of her disappearance, every street post and storefront bore her photograph. The paper had faded but the photograph captured the wide, glassy coves of the girl's eyes. People were searching for her. They combed the countryside as far north as Lisbon and south to where the land concedes to sea. On television, the girl's parents addressed the press. Their voices fell mute against the waves of café chimes. I watched the girl's mother. Her face was pale and sullen; her movements held taut an invisible line of hope. Her lips outlined her pleas. But words, too, go lost in the current.

The Portuguese use the word *saudade* for the things that seem unspeakable. In English, we have no direct translation of the word, perhaps because its complexity of emotion is unmatched, at once beautiful and heartbreaking—an essence suspended between remembrance and longing, nostalgia and the buried knowledge that what we long for may never return.

We fought before I left home, my mother and I. We still fight the way we did when I was a girl: with the catch and release of silence. She worries when I leave, even now. I ignore her concern, recasting the lines of my adulthood. There is an inevitable sense of loss, of leaving things behind that comes with traveling—a loss that perhaps also comes with growing up. I know no words to translate the feel of pressing my cheek against the smooth surface of my mother's arm. *Saudade.* My mother is silver and turquoise in Mexico, a pair of shiny castanets in Spain. There in the Algarve, my mother was a trace of scales, mere glitter on my fingertips.

I cradled a sardine in my hand. The brine and oil bled into the bread just as the light shone through the window, through the poster of the missing girl, which thinned like a gauzy curtain. A group of schoolgirls passed by, saddle shoes clipping in a hopscotch rhythm along the church steps. Two of them stopped at the window. Their eyes hardened for an instant. One girl tugged at a strand of her hair. As they skipped away, their navy skirt pleats pinwheeled behind them.

And there, along the rim of my plate, flakes of skin and frail bones had dried translucent, gray. As I awaited my bill, I wondered after Saint Anthony, how in a matter of days the locals would celebrate him as they did each year, praying for miracles, offering bread, grilling fish like the ones I ate that day: fish with silver, crepe-paper skin that sheds to expose a tender, sea-salted meat. Tender, like the flesh of a mother's arms, still waiting for her child to find home.

To Capture the Castle

If it were not for landscape, I would know nothing of faith. Every year, thousands flock to Croagh Patrick on Reek Sunday in July, making the twenty-five-hundred-foot trek to hear mass on the summit, where Saint Patrick fasted and prayed for the conversion of the Irish nation. I arrived at the mountain, just east of Westport in County Mayo, during the second week of an extended road trip through Ireland, traveling not alone, as I often did, but with my mother, who, while gazing up at a stone statue of the devoutly Catholic saint said to have conquered Celtic belief, seemed to remember that it was the twenty-first of June.

"Today is the solstice," she said. "The longest day of the year."

I am unnerved by the recognition that when I arrived in Ireland, I was happy, at least in part because of the misconception that yet again I was moving, traveling far from things I knew—the everyday actions like riding the subway or stopping at the grocery store—the routine reminders that I was living in my mother's apartment with no money and no job, trying to get my mind right after having come out on the other side of a few rough years. By then I had scaled enough mountains to know never to doubt the challenge of a climb or the breathtaking reward. So I approached the mountain, with its three stations of prayer, blessed by an intrepid and earnest inquiry into the nature of pilgrimage.

I. Leacht Benáin

It was nearly five o'clock when we began to climb. Most people we passed were already heading down, their exhausted, limping figures nearly lost beneath their expressions—something between joy and relief at having returned to sturdy ground. The well-worn path, its edges clad in shrubs and purple heather, lay uneven beneath our feet but was easily navigable and soon turned to alternating beds of quartzite and schist. My mother took the lead, great naturalist that she is, snapping photographs, noting the flora, keeping pace with her excitement. I fell into stride close behind her but dallied, crisscrossing the trail as a dog might, owning the slowness of my steps—my pace beholden to the wildflowers, which across the country were in bloom. Several hundred feet above, people appeared like chess pieces against the middle ridge, bishops and rooks, kings and queens dancing on the stage of sky.

Weeks earlier we had visited Glenveagh Castle nestled among the lakes of eastern Donegal, and ever since, I had been thinking about how castles are like mountains. A castle may be anything from a prehistoric mound or hill fort to a crenellated mansion. They serve as strongholds in times of trouble. Once palatial shelters of kings and noble lords, castles are now preserved as monuments and museums, shrines bearing testament to the past, much like how we build and maintain memory in the spirit of self-preservation.

On the trail ahead, a middle-aged couple stood at the edge of the path. My mother waved as she passed, her legs bounding upward. I was a few yards away when I saw the slumped curve of their backs, the locked jaws of their stalemate. The man seemed to be waiting for the woman's next move. He gestured toward the summit and then back to the trailhead. His movements were kind, conciliatory, perhaps futile, but patient. We exchanged quiet greetings as I passed. The woman's eyes, fixed and swollen, gazed toward the ocean view.

Trying to catch up with my mother, I found myself willing the couple on. The trail had grown rocky, but the incline was still manageable, so I imagined how, once they resumed the trail, we would cross paths again, perhaps as they reached the summit and I began my descent.

Earlier that day, I had read about an archaeological excavation of Croagh Patrick in the mid-1990s that confirmed evidence of early Christian activity on the mountain but also revealed (with the help of radiocarbon dating) that the site was important during the pre-Christian era. For thousands of years people walked the same trail. That alone seemed as much a reason to continue up the reek as the promise of a spectacular view. Still, I sensed that the couple had reached an impasse I might never understand.

I've never felt a spiritual devotion. My father, though he doesn't talk much about it, has his own form of faith, I'm sure. Before I was born, he was enrolled in Gordon-Conwell, a theological seminary outside of Boston, but (while that may have been where he first encountered the biblical name he would choose for me) art seemed to be his ultimate calling. My mother, braless and batiked until the late 1980s, leaned toward folk traditions. We sent "peace cards" on Christmas; we lit candles on the solstice. But for years, my curiosity about religious faith wouldn't quit.

Soon I reached a large mound of stones set off from the trail, *Leacht Benáin*, named for one of Saint Patrick's disciples. A small plaque listed the penitential exercises that earn forgiveness of sins: *Walk seven times around the mound of stones while reciting seven Our Fathers, seven Hail Marys, one Creed.*

I had seen this, the way the pilgrims circle in prayer, in footage from the annual climb featured on a news report a few years before. It rained that year, and the people in hooded ponchos and trail shoes walked slowly with hiking sticks, circling the stones, the rhythm of their steps and muted recitations lost in the fog.

I walked once around the mound of stones, trying to get a sense of its size. And then I remembered I had seen the circling once before. When I was twenty-two and fell ill in a Guatemalan village, the children in the orphanage where I stayed had prayed, their toes scuffing and catching on each other's heels as they circled my bed.

I rejoined the path and tried to spot my mother, who had made ground up the reek. She appeared as a speck against the terrain, like the chess pieces I had seen from the base—knights, maidens, pawns, triumphant at the midpoint of their climb. And I remembered a boy I had known since kindergarten, when everything was sandboxes and skinned knees, and was in love with by the third grade, despite our separate desk groups. He had died in a car crash in southern California just months before I left for Ireland, and all I could think about was how we went to see Medieval Times on his ninth birthday. Inside the stone walls of Lyndhurst Castle, a life-size replication, somewhere in New Jersey, of an eleventh-century barracks, six knights in authentic armor clashed in a jousting tournament for the title of King's Champion. We cheered for the Red and Yellow Knight, eating chicken off the bone, drinking chalices of orange soda, believing we were nobles of the court.

Ahead, two more figures: a woman leading a young man. They descended in slow procession. Carrying a small pack and a walking stick, the woman, just an arm's reach in front of the man, looked back every two feet or so, as if checking that he was still there. I slowed my pace, suddenly aware of the sound of my steps against the scree, the stones clinking and scraping as my feet sunk into the shallow rock bed. As they neared, the woman's face looked gentle. The young man trailed her. His eyes were glued to the ground as his weight, buckling with each step, hung on his walking staff. His feet were bare but for a thin pair of socks worn through at the toe and heel and stained with blood. A coat of dust extended up to his knees. The air felt tight, as if the sky held its breath.

II. The Summit

The trail broadened into a collection of rocks that scarred the mountain. The stones shifting beneath my feet sounded like ice cubes in a tumbler. Without realizing, as my mind wandered and my stride lengthened, I had passed my mother and was leading us. Not far above, I saw the saddle ridge, which offered some relief, as the climb had grown steep. After charging several paces upward to reach the ridge, I leaned back to keep my balance on the steep angle of the trail. The view stretched clear across Clew Bay's deep water scattered with silvery green islands. I wondered if the shoeless penitent had stopped here to rest his feet, if the beauty uplifted and ushered him on. Would it lead us to fortitude? Is there a place for earthly incentive in the path of sacrifice?

I was unprepared for the final ascent. The air cooled; the path grew steep. My feet sank into the rocks. Small boulders stacked at a near vertical angle no longer bore handholds. I stepped slowly, strategically, at several points lowering to my hands and knees to crawl. The wind clamored like a percussive snare drum in my ears—the music of procession, of pomp and circumstance. I braced against the rocks, and the touch of them sparked memory: my friends and I, as children, pressing our palms and fingers together to compare hands, and then splaying them against the rock wall of granite and Manhattan schist; the fortified courtyard where we played taps at recess; the fenced-in park where we rolled joints and traded secrets. Against the rock I can see the years my hands grew bony, tipped with chipped middle-school manicures, and then long and veined like my mother's.

A boy, barely eight or nine, emerged from the summit. Extending one foot at a time, he tested the rocks before placing his step, and then pivoted, hand outstretched. Behind him, a thin elderly man appeared all skin and bones in a tweed suit and carrying a cane. His limbs wobbled as he grasped the boy's arm. I stood aside to give them room enough to pass, steadying myself between two rocks. The man nodded. His skin, folded and creased, looked translucent. I bowed slightly in the wind.

The two of them seemed to glide over the same boulders that I, short-breathed, clung to clumsily. As if descending a staircase the sky itself had offered, they disappeared down the mountain as steadily as they had come.

Neither the highest nor the hardest of climbs, Croagh Patrick offered more a sense of panoramic wonder. A dramatic view of Clew Bay and the Nephin Beg mountains to the north can be seen from the summit. When I reached the top, the wind whipped around my head and neck. The air at that height, in its all-encompassing breeze, felt like riding in the back of a pickup truck at full speed down the highway—the world too much to take in, the air too abundant to breathe.

I wanted to say a prayer, but I didn't know where to begin. Even the Hail Marys and Our Fathers that I knew, most of which I had learned in Spanish from the children in Río Dulce, seemed all wrong. Instead, I walked over to a small mound of stones and read the plaque of instructions: *Kneel and say seven Our Fathers, seven Hail Marys, one Creed. Pray near the chapel for the Pope's intentions.*

I imagined the movements outlined on the signpost and pictured a courtly yet humble dance of minstrels and troubadours. Who wrote these lines? Who issued these directives? I am fascinated by ritual— this instruction through ceremony or tradition that holds people in a place of faith, a sense of communal belonging that has structure, directions, a map, perhaps, for the soul.

I turned back to the trail edge and watched my mother's head crown from below. She pulled herself up the last step of the trail and then stopped, squinting toward the bay, and joined me. We circled the summit chapel, which glowed white and warm, and kept rotating, trying to get our cardinal bearings. I wondered how we appeared from below, tiny pieces moving on an elaborate game board.

Not quite able to place where I'm from, people sometimes ask about my childhood and then seem surprised to learn that I'm from a big city, surprised by the rough edges I contain, the accent and slang that sometimes falls in drunken slurs from my mouth—a little bit hip-hop, a little bit Yiddish. It's hard to explain how it feels to have grown up in extremes, to connect to others in pieces of the self, and how those pieces become like relics. There are no explanations for the things that we preserve as sacred: imagination and curiosity, castles and knights, dollhouses and make-believe, the people and places we love and remain intrinsically attached to even if our attachment determines us to leave. Saint Patrick left his home, his freedom from captivity, to return to Ireland and the people who enslaved him in order to answer a voice—a calling that governed his life and legend. Edna O'Brien left the land she called home to live in exile. The peace she obtained living abroad let her more clearly depict her homeland's grace and influence. When Yeats left Thoor Ballylee, the castle where he wrote his famous tower poems, he wrote, "to leave here is to leave beauty behind."

My mother began building a cairn to commemorate our climb, and I joined her. Several piles lay scattered around the chapel. Balancing one stone at a time, we constructed a stack. My mother placed two buds of purple heather beneath the top stone.

"To the solstice," she said. It wasn't a prayer, but it was a gesture we knew. I imagined the saints at a loss, celestial kings and bishops rolling in their graves.

III. Roilig Mhuire
The descent proved an almost greater challenge to navigate as each step sunk into the tumbling scree, and more than once I took to an inverted crawl, like a jester or a sand crab scurrying down a dune. When we reached the saddle once again, I was relieved to know we had passed the steepest part. The ridge stretched serpentine before us, the view extended on both sides, and for the first time—though I wondered why I hadn't seen it on the way up—I caught a glimpse of the back end of the ridge, where the mountain slope was dappled

with more rock signs and cairns. Some resembled initials framed in hearts—the ruins of testimonials, a marriage proposal, the skeletal alignment of letters. Many of the stones were now gone, perhaps pillaged for another's communiqué: messages to God, a lover, fellow hill-walkers, tourists and travelers who have made the climb, the mountaineers and trail runners to whom Croagh Patrick is perhaps but a small summit among hundreds. I had seen the same tokens at the summit. At a small plot marked for Saint Patrick's bed, icons and rosaries tied with wildflowers lay nestled in the dirt along with handwritten messages and photographs. Prayers weighted down by stones: a woman longing for a child, a boy sent off to fight in the war, a girl who is ill, another who is lost.

Every belief has a story. Every story has a setting. Perhaps the sacred is not entirely intangible. Perhaps landscape, or place, is integral to belief. Religious conflicts have for years persisted over disputed lands—mere outlines and boundaries. We know where relics lie throughout the world, where holy water flows, where saints and martyrs rest. Our religious texts are as much historical records as they are relics of cartography, which is why people journey to Bethlehem, Damascus, Santiago de Compostela in Spain, or the western shores of County Mayo. Somewhere in southern California there is a tree by a road that bore the point of impact that killed my childhood friend. There is a sidewalk in the Bronx that absorbed the blood of my first true fall. Somewhere in the East Village is a church where I first tried to pray.

I can understand pilgrimage as an act that asks the body to journey for the soul. To summit a mountain, to complete a trail, to reach an ancient monument offers a tangible sense of arrival. The worn and weary legs of a pilgrim are but a physical expression. The old man led by the young boy I could only imagine to be his grandson knew this. The young man with his torn, bloodied socks hobbling over the rocks knew this. But what of the couple stopped in despair? I never saw them again as we made our way back down the reek. Was it their knees aching beneath the constantly shifting rocks, or a lack of imagination, spiritual stamina—of faith—to see through their climb?

At the time I might have denied that faith had anything to do with my sense of belonging on that mountain, but I couldn't ignore the sense that the mountain itself, and all of the living and dying that it held, recognized my grief: grief for the way we ration hope as we grow up, hardening like armor as the flowers and make-believe fall from our garlanded heads. Despite the hurt and longing, summiting the reek offered the bewildering sense that the world was as it should be, that I had taken part in something, albeit something I may never understand.

After some time, along the center of the saddle ridge, we reach the final station, Roilig Mhuire, the Virgin's Cemetery, a set of three large boulder cairns that rests some ways down the western slope. A plaque nestled in the rock pile bears instructions for the final station: *Walk seven times around each mound of stones saying seven Our Fathers, seven Hail Marys, one Creed. Walk seven times around the whole enclosure of Roilig Mhuire praying.*

I looked back at my mother, her fair skin flushed from the climb, her eyes as blue as the sky behind her. At my feet a purple flower appeared by the side of the trail, just as I had seen the same amethyst crowns at my feet by Glenveagh Castle. We continued on toward sturdy ground, savoring the light of the longest of days.

In its own way, this climb was a plea; this mountain, a prayer. Just as a Benediction is recited, a rosary worried, a candle lit, we summit a peak, we build a cairn, and we are no longer where we started. I didn't set forth to climb Croagh Patrick with the perspective of a pilgrim, nor offer penance as I walked its path. But didn't my stride at some point become more deliberate? Didn't my thoughts dissipate into a stream of consciousness perpetuated by my legs, my pulse, my breath? When we journey, we learn, like catechism, our own instructions. We find a mountain. We find a castle. We touch all of the exquisite stones and wildflowers on earth—dub every last one of them: great sinners, great penitents and pilgrims, yes. Rooks and queens and bishops, too. Mothers and daughters, childhood friends. The gracious, the skeptics, the saved.

L'Éternelle Idole

A Chapter on Red

It is not the form that dictates the color,
but the color that brings out the form.
HANS HOFMANN

First: a heart, or three, drawn and cut from construction paper. Nearly twice the size of my hand, so that when I held them, waiting for my mother, they balanced weightless on my palm. My mother knelt with a handful of pins pursed between her lips. One by one, she adhered the hearts in a row down the front of my dress: above the bottom hem, at my waistline, at the center of my chest. A tissue-paper crown and glittery staff completed my coronation. Released into the hallowed night I yelled, "Off with their heads!" as I trailed the superhero cape of my older brother through the echoing hallways of our Bronx apartment building in search of tricks or treats. How easy it seemed to craft something lovely from paper and scissors—and a heart, no less, so perfectly trimmed, at once sharp-edged and smooth in triptych against my white cotton gown.

———

Or perhaps, even before the hearts, there was Matisse. I would sit before a small reproduction of Matisse's *The Red Studio* that hung in my parents' bedroom, which, when the futon was folded away, was also the living room. For the longest time, I thought Matisse's studio must be a room in a dollhouse—somewhere the Queen herself might reside. Awash in Venetian red, the canvas depicts what the artist must have seen before him as he worked—a still life of propped paintings and sculptures. The artworks, rendered in detail and color, are indicated only by negative gaps in the red surface. Of his painting Matisse once remarked, "I find that all these things . . . only become what they are to me when I see them together with the color red." A grandfather clock stands in the center of the composition. Matisse eliminated its hands, as if, in the space of the artist's studio, time is suspended. As if all attention were given to the process of seeing a retrospective housed in a single color.

———

"It might help you better relax," my father told me as he tried to explain an exercise he learned in art school to focus the mind on a single color and every instance in which it occurs. "Try red," he said. And because often my father's ideas have a way of taking root in my mind as a steady preoccupation, I try his exercise. On my way to work I take inventory: traffic lights, stop signs, a fire engine. A tinsel holiday wreath tied and forgotten on a telephone pole. An array of lipsticks and nail polish, headscarves and jewelry. The laces of a young boy's tennis shoes. The looped handle of a baby's rattle. And just when it seems the world is alive in red, the cat that sleeps on floor of the neighborhood bodega slinks lazily from around a corner with a fresh bead of blood on its whiskers, as if to remind us coffee-and-cigarette "regulars" that something is always dying.

It isn't long before my catalog of red inhabits the mind—integrating and then segregating memory through a siphon of red. I see the construction-paper hearts. I see the wheels of my roller skates, the bright handlebars of the new bicycle I first rode without training wheels along the Hudson, the deep chrome of the vintage Schwinn I found at a thrift store in Colorado—and between those two bicycles alone, there are twenty-some-odd years to color in.

Can I tell a story in a single color? The painters did it: Rothko and Hofmann. Yves Klein, too (but he may better serve an essay on blue). Can we fulfill our memories in monochrome? Bathe words in color as Matisse dared bathe his canvas?

———

Before I saw, I tasted. When I was eight years old playing catch with my brother, I ran for the ball and within an instant lay flat on the ground with a mouthful of concrete. My two front teeth (the new adult teeth of which I was so proud) lay somewhere in the salty mess that unfolded in my mouth. The bitter taste, like a penny splintered and molten along my tongue, churned against my raw gums. I hardly registered what happened—that I had tripped on the sidewalk's uneven pavement. But I made the catch that day. I remember only because of how tightly I gripped the ball, refusing to let go. Even as my brother and the neighbors came running; even as my father took me inside, shielding my eyes from the bathroom mirror as he cleaned my wounds. My face and hands and knees throbbed for days. As I healed, my friends came to see the new front teeth my dentist fashioned from caps of enamel around the ruins of my incisors. My brother brought his friends by after school to show off, like a crime scene, the place where my face stained the sidewalk, which was little more than an inkblot or splattering of paint. And yet it recorded, like evidence, my first lesson in glory and pain, of how quickly we fall between the two, how humbled we become by our own missteps.

I was even younger, six or seven, when I learned of the birds. The hummingbirds were my favorite. The ruby-throated in particular, the one variety most likely to stray east of the Mississippi, so I waited for them to visit New York. When I discovered they were attracted to red, I became consumed, concocting nectar from sugar water and food coloring. I filled feeders and mason jars and placed them on the windowsills and fire escape.

Most bird-pollinated flowers are red and rich in nectar. But is this simply because the honeybees can't decipher them? How odd that the color red, which at the end of the spectrum carries the longest wave of light, is inconspicuous to the bees, and therefore left for the birds. Imagine a male cardinal—so effortlessly designed to attract—appearing to a yellow jacket as little more than a notion against the bare winter trees and snow.

This, my first lesson in matters of the birds and bees: color holds the power to entice and allure. And since then, I have seen it countless times in the plucked look skin has when touched by frost or wind or sun, when flushed with sex or panic or desire. Like the scarf-flaunting matadors in Spain courting their bulls. Or the rose of the flamenco dancer, following the rhythmic clap of her castanets. Like the polish I'm never bold enough to wear on my fingernails, the lipstick I've never cared for, the blush I find laughable because my cheeks redden on their own, under even the slightest pretense.

Summer afternoons, I got in the habit of eating pomegranates with the boy next door. He was the son of our Greek landlady, a woman who spat over my head and told me I was beautiful. Raised in a world of secular bohemia, I found unending curiosity in Greek Orthodox traditions. We'd sit on the back porch, each with our orb, pulling at its tough rind, breaking into it as if into a crystal ball that held secrets we wanted nothing more than to devour. We brushed the juice from our fingers onto our bare knees. The color took to our skin like watercolor. The jeweled kernels, ruby arils, burst in my mouth, their flavor like the first boy I kissed. The first boy I swore on instinct to love, and failed to.

This was the same fruit the landlady had us smash against our doorstep before the first stride across the threshold on New Year's morning. And like the red-dyed egg nestled in the bread we ate the night before, it was a mark of fortune and safety.

Now, in the town where I live, the locals raise Chinese lanterns along Main Street to mark the new year. But I'm still curious about pomegranates. I still raise one to my nose each year as I pass them in the grocery store. What children are sitting on back steps courting sweetness? How many stride over doorsteps where the same fruit juice has seeped into stone, dried, and grown sticky in the sun? The mark of another year, broken open, promising to be new.

———

A friend of mine, a florist in town, once gave me a lesson in roses. Deep reds signify burning passion, she told me, while lighter hues mean romance. Crimson is the color of sex (which, she takes time to explain, is different from romance) and not to be confused with burgundy, which connotes desire. The symbolism is accredited, she assures me. But I have my doubts. Didn't the ancient Greeks believe roses came from the blood of Adonis and were as much symbolic of love and affinity as of growth and decay? What about red chrysanthemums—one of the four Noble Gentlemen who mark the seasons in the East? Or the poppies for remembrance that line the castles in Ireland? I find more enchantment in lilacs and wildflowers. We don't order bouquets for wit or humor. Not enough people send flowers for valor and distinction.

the duality of 'red'

———

I wasn't surprised to learn that in 1949, the same year that Matisse's painting of his studio subsumed in a field of cadmium went on view at New York's Museum of Modern Art, Mark Rothko began exploring abstraction by painting soft-edged blocks in diaphanous colors.

Of Matisse's canvas, Rothko said: "When you looked at that painting, you became that color, you became totally saturated with it." And this seems more or less to explain Rothko's own process for addressing his work, the way he seemed to will or breathe the paint onto his canvases in a slow spinning of reds and yellows, like gossamer, like screens. In a painting we expect such color to last, to be present, as long as we care to notice. But what—I want to say to Rothko as I try to saturate these pages—what happens when color fades?

———

For centuries, red was the treasure of the Incas and Aztecs, and then the wealth of red belonged to Spain. When it is fresh, carmine pigment, made from the bodies of cochineal beetles, is one of the purest dyes produced in the natural world. But it is also the most fleeting.

J. M. W. Turner painted with carmine even though he knew of its impermanence. And so his work, his bequest to the nation of England, was far more colorful than the signature gray stormscapes we see today. Imagine an artist trying to capture the moment of a setting sun unleashing a brilliant slash of light through the clouds. As he reached to dip his brush, how could he not choose the best pigment, the perfect red, even though he knew it wouldn't last? What if words became illegible after they were written? Wouldn't we write them all the same? Unconcerned with posterity, Turner cared little of a painting's longevity but of the very moment it was created. Red, vanishing and evanescent, was his immediate—near fugitive—desire.

———

When I was eighteen and moved west to Colorado, I thought I would mourn the east coast foliage. My mother sent care packages filled with origami cranes and folded stars, nestled in a bed of pressed maple leaves. "Pieces of home," she called them, as if titling a shadow box or still life. But "home" has always been a variable. And some years ago, when I finally left Colorado and returned to the Northeast, it was the red rock canyons I craved.

I prefer red in its organic incarnations—rust-red creek beds, sea oats, and sumac leaves, the blooms of algae that color the Red Sea. But the human hand that paints in red or the manufactured, commissioned varieties of red satisfy my belief in the duality of things. We have co-opted the natural shades of fruits and flowers and assigned them to passion, to seduction, and—be it forbidden or sanctioned—to love. Pigments and paints are poised to accentuate and allure. And yet we color stop signs and fire engines red. Emergency exits and security warnings all bear the color of fear and trepidation—of warning. Waves of taillights and the flashing lights of emergency vehicles color tragic nights.

No wonder then that the reason some stones appear red is the same reason our blood runs red: iron colors human and earthly temperament. Science teaches this. But what about the stories and myths we tell ourselves, the meaning we make, in order to endure? According to Iroquois legend, after three hunters killed the Great Bear, the animal's blood fell from the sky to color the leaves. And because I learned this in elementary school, in the portable planetarium our science teacher erected in the gymnasium, and because the image still haunts me as beautiful, it is the story I will tell my children if ever they are born: that death and demise often lead to splendor. Red is the dying leaves, just as dying stars exhibit a Mars-like tint before they go—evidence of their passing, yet just as much evidence of their life.

Before death, there will forever be the injuries of love. The first: my father, who broke the bones in his hand against a table as my parents negotiated their divorce. The second: my first love, who caught a ricocheting shard from the glass he threw against the wall on the eve of our inevitable split. His ring finger, nearly severed, glistened scarlet to the bone. And though he was the patient in the hospital emergency room, my whole body ached as if I had fallen, pieces of me lost upon impact, calcified, dislodged. I would ache this way for years after, recoil at the thought of the raw vacancy, the bare tissue. And again, the markings, this time left shamefully on the carpet and on the pillowcase I used to wrap his hand. The color dried and deepened to rustic burgundy—wasn't that my florist's term for desire? Or was it the earthy red of van Gogh's severed despair after Gauguin threatened to leave him? Far from the fleeting flush of a lover's heaving chest, when we cut our bonds such injuries stain. Red is the color of love and lunacy, of infatuation and its failure, of how slowly, tolerantly—as if in a pact of silence—we drift between the two.

When I look up the word red, I find its origin in the Indo-European ruedh, and later the Greek erythros. In Sanskrit, rakta is the word used for *red* and for blood. In Comanche, the word *ekapi* is used for *red* and color and circle, too, which suggests something fundamental, something all-encompassing. Red is the color of beauty in Russia, of luck and good fortune in China. It is the color of Greek tragedies, epic battles of glory and salvation. Ancient Romans painted their gladiators and heroes in red; they washed the statues of gods and emperors with the same ruddy pigments that can be found in the murals of Pompeii. Here, we might gossip over red-carpet celebrities and in the same breath recall catching a red-handed thief. We might anticipate the pomp and circumstance of a red-letter day as much as we curse the red herring of deceit. We hang flags of patriotism and revolution, landmark districts of prostitution and lust.

———

We say *red-eye* and we mean flying overnight. But it is also what I call crying until morning. The kind of weeping—silent, full—that might be reserved for blue, except that it hoods our lids and circles the underside of the eye in red. The kind of weeping I learned from my mother, the kind you wake to the next morning and nurse like jetlag or a hangover, face puffed, swollen, a little older around the eyes. The red of rage and grief and euphoric sadness; the red-eye of weightlessness, of rebirth.

———

Or maybe it's the dim tint of an evening bar, which used to lure me, like a moth toward light. Nights after all my friends retired into taxicabs and slinked away to their Brooklyn apartments, I wandered the city looking for clues into unexplained grief, and found the inevitable cliché cocktailed in the pouty stranger at the end of the bar who, once we had stumbled back to his apartment, showed me his paintings—all brooding drips and globs that, in the dark, hinted at kindness. He went on and on about the New York School until I threatened to leave. When I did slip away, the air a little bit pink as it turned heavily to day, the metal door to his walkup that shut forcefully behind me—a door that still floats like a buoy in the shadowy sea of the Bowery—was solid and padlocked and red.

———

While on the subject of doors, let this serve as an entryway into my memory of the red-doored church in the old neighborhood—landmark of my greatest curiosities, my greatest shame—that I used to circle as a girl, trying to learn something, waiting for its sober advice. In many cities, houses of faith and worship are marked by similar doors signifying safe haven. Once, Hebrew slaves were instructed to brush lamb's blood on their doors to protect their firstborn. Catholic churches paint their front doors red, the blood of Christ and martyrs, to mark the borders of holy ground, the threshold where physical or spiritual harm could not penetrate, where pursuers could pursue no further. The red of sanctuary and protection.

―――――――

If I were to return to—if I were to safeguard or time capsule—one image of red, it would be the paper hearts, royal insignia of my girlhood make-believe and the simplicity of young desire. My brother and I paraded as our heroes—he alternating between Superman and Captain America, me reluctantly assigned to Wonder Woman—a fantastical duo with hearts primed to save the world. Or a single queen ready to issue the brutal destiny of beheaded hope. And if those hearts seem too naive, perhaps, instead, a package of red doilies I bought in college at a thrift shop—the same shop with the stunning vintage Schwinn— that I strung into lacy curtains, still believing in paper-made pleasures. And they lasted, too, nearly as long as that first bout of love, before the wind took them. I think sometimes of their fate, wonder what bird may have swooped up their shreds to insulate its nest, what child discovered them littering the sidewalk during a game of catch, how the paper crimped and fell to the ground like fresh autumn leaves.

―――――――

The next time I visit my father, I tell him I no longer see things the same. And to some extent, that's true. Color seems more evident now, more laden with testimony, with consequence. "Try red," my father had said. So simple. And now I notice it everywhere: in the cranberries and rhubarb stalks at the farmers' market, the cider apples and bell peppers, and yes, the pomegranates, too. In the book bindings that wall the library, the neon sign kept on at the diner, or the historic brick buildings that accentuate downtown.

Of course the painters knew not only how color is revealed in form, but how form—a synthesis of light and reflection—is just as much revealed in color. In the city, sirens sound and lights flash through the streets delivering their cargo of pain and sadness: a nineteen-year-old who took one in the gut on Heath Avenue after holding the door for some thug's sister, leaving behind the red pool that must have swelled beneath him—the stain of chivalry's passing. But what if the sirens and lights signify a heart being rushed for transplant, or an expectant mother about to birth her only child? The fire engines rush too, and a family may have lost their house, but what if a child is rescued from a fearful height or a battered home? Stalled traffic lights on Broadway mean frustrated commuters, waiting. But they also mean more time to breathe—stillness in a frenzied city.

———

"Color has taken possession of me," Paul Klee once said of his work. His canvases reveal color and shapes—stick figures and fish, houses and hearts—in a childlike, sophisticated meditation.

Here we begin and end again with the heart, because what greater possession exists? Not just in color, not simply through this red (by which I mean rose-colored) lens, but as it adheres and tears, as it is pinned and stripped bare. It may be an impossible idea, to tell the story of a color, but perhaps we might glimpse a chapter that contains a single human experience, a retrospective of memory, the folded edges of paper and pleasure and pain, tucked into a chamber, a studio, a cabinet of curiosity. When oxygenated, when exposed, it pulses in crimson and scarlet, carmine, red—at once the longest wavelength of visible light and the first color we lose sight of at twilight.

On Grazing

Bos primigenius
PUEBLO, COLORADO

I used to collect things: rocks and minerals, artifacts and molds. That afternoon we ditched English lit and sociology to flee to the tracks where we hopped a train toward the southwestern plains, only to hop off again somewhere—anywhere—to spoon beans from a can, sip whiskey from a canteen, and suckle and knead each other's flesh because we were sweethearts and the world was alive. That afternoon, we almost missed a set of antlers, dropped like driftwood—a discarded shield or scepter—a buck's fallen crown, bone smooth and half-buried in the gravel.

———

A recollection: Although young, I knew what death was, could sense foul play in the dampness of the barnyard beneath the cover of fresh hay. Although I never saw the headlines—"9 Farm Pets Found Mutilated on a School Campus in the Bronx"—I knew the story was more than what we were told when the herd of us (six-and-a-halfs and almost-tens) arrived at camp that day or what was later overheard: "suspect at large" after fleeing the scene of a crime termed "brutal but not ritualistic," as if there were solace in that. I wonder if he thought, before he slaughtered the final lamb, "This is the final lamb." Or if he noticed the names we had chosen, carved into wooden plaques and nailed above their stalls, before he escaped into the night with his cruelty and his stains, perhaps hopping a train headed south toward the city or north toward anywhere else.

———

An inquiry: Maybe this is where my obsession with captivity—or rather freedom and abandon—began. That summer at camp we learned to care for the animals, to save our lunch scraps for the pig bucket, to milk the goats, to cradle the rabbits until we felt their hearts slow in our arms. That summer I fell in love with Saint Francis, swore I might one day live in Assisi or somewhere where the sky wasn't so confined, caught between the concrete and steel of the city, the trees and longing of the boroughs—neighborhoods of bad prospect and saturated urban soils.

———

A *keepsake*: In our nakedness by the fire, this lover and I take turns holding the antlers above our heads, dirt from the rugged bone leaving smudges on our foreheads. I remember as a girl posing for photographs between the animal ears at the Bronx Zoo, squatting, and then rising into the opening where the head of a jackrabbit or moose might belong, all of which may have taught me something about transience and the frailty of ideals, of how to pull myself up into the body of a boxcar, live for a moment in the hollow heart of a freight train, then bound back into the world unharmed.

———

That night in the pasture, deserted but for the junipers and the cooling embers of our bodies, I kept waking up wondering if the animals knew of our trespass, thinking my chest might be trampled beneath a cow's hoof, my ribs crushed by the gaze of a mare. But we left the antlers by the tracks before making camp, kept the fire low and our lovemaking quiet. And more than my anxiety about the cows, what troubled me most was a nagging curiosity: What makes us different from animal or machine—the ability to forgive? Guilt? Sorrow? Meanness?

———

A *relic*: Because the crime went unsolved, it has weighed on me a strand of questions: How did he manage to jump the fence, break the barn door's padlock, and stab and crush the animals, leaving the carcasses for the groundskeeper to find before the hundred of us children arrived, leaving the news for the adults to spin into story? Did he know I would never believe it? The absence lingered in the hosed-off ground like a footprint that the police might have missed and traced to a hiking boot, a pair he borrowed from his father, or that were a Christmas gift from his mom. Why do goats still break my heart? Why can I never look them fully in the eye?

A confession: I have harbored a hatred for this stranger since I was a girl. I would like to say that it comes from a noble commitment to justice, a rage against animal cruelty. But more, I resent him for the way he has made me wary of having children. Can I be so bold as to hang the cross of doubt and uncertainty on this nameless antagonist? If so, what else can I allege? What other charges can I shoulder onto his rap sheet? My drunkenness? My bad judgment? My obsession with youth? I empathize with the parts of us that make us do the things we do. It is the silent repercussions that I despise—the way each jab of his knife tore tiny wounds in our hearts, how each neck he bludgeoned and snapped made our wide eyes irrevocably squint toward the world. For that I have struggled to find ways of saying, "I forgive you."

Or maybe I haven't even tried. I still visit farms and leave the pen doors unlatched, just in case the animals need an escape, just in case he still hunts barnyards, posing as a father or an uncle at an unfenced playground. Would he do it all over again? Or might the air carry the chug of a boxcar so he'd run instead, see the gleam of the tracks, find the spokes of a wheel and time his jump?

———

A kind of mercy: In the morning I woke beneath the same junipers, the same sky, the same embers cooling as ash, and everywhere the fog had settled so it was hard to make out the congregation of cows that had gathered at dawn. I had feared they would trample us, brand our skin, leave us praying to our saints and repenting all our sins. But they stepped slowly around us, their edges blurring in the mist. One of them stood not more than a few inches away. My heart stilled. The cow chewed steadily on the dry grass, churning its cud, its tail whipping gently. And the boy next to me never knew they were there, still swears it must have been a dream: the way I reached out, touched my fingertips against the cow's coarse flank and thigh, flattened my hand on its warm hide, felt its pulse against my palm, breathing the same air: air that had grown thinner, more temperate, in the rising fog.

A Theory of Substance

Concrete

In 2007, at the Tate Modern's Turbine Hall, the artist Doris Salcedo installed a crack in the floor. In an exhibition space normally filled with architectural sculptures and towering constructions—once a model of the sun—no one was quite sure how the crack was made. The installation, titled *Shibboleth*, began as a hairline fracture in the concrete slab floor and gradually, and then all of a sudden, deepened into a three-foot crevasse (ten inches at its widest point) that meandered and branched out through the space.

Sand

I think often about that line, which had no apparent origin. I think, too, about all of the seams and perimeters we contain, like the line my brother marked down the center of our shared bedroom as kids, the way certain streets partition entire neighborhoods—the 125th Street divide between Harlem and the Upper East Side, peace lines segregating urban streets in Ireland between Catholic and Protestant—how a line painted on a city bus could fuel protests and arrests in Birmingham. On one side is the physical world where we meet our desires with propriety and control. On the other, an abandonment of intent, a surrendering to what lies beneath the surface. The roughness of sand can smooth the hardest marble. The texture of a nylon stocking gets caught on the smallest inconsistencies of skin, like the wrong direction velvet contains. At the Villa Borghese in Rome, circling the bare ass of Apollo, I can see the single moment that defines the young god's pursuit of Daphne, two figures captured at the brink of their fate—he reaching her at the very point she turns forever into a tree, both rooting and leaving before him.

Flesh

I imagine the last summer we lived together on San Juan Island as a slow splintering of edges we tried again and again to smooth. Those days I woke early, stepping outside our small trailer with its peeling blue finish, into the early dampness, stretching like an animal—sinewy, unkempt—my hair coiled and blonde, my skin the shade of late June, when the darkness of my tan made highlights of the faint scars along the inner bend of my wrist. Bedding down in the sunspots of the wooded clearing, I felt warm pine needles brush beneath my back. I had heard of a new fawn seen isolated in the woods while the doe mother foraged nearby. In a half sleep, I listened for them, imagining the fawn trying to blend into the world until it grew stronger and gained strength to stand.

Cedar

Joe dragged a stack of shingles from the shed. I grabbed the tools. We were reshingling the side of an old garage barn for his mother in order to make extra money before we made our way back east. With most of the lower sections already complete, Joe and a neighbor had rigged scaffolding so we could reach the upper walls. Earlier that summer we had begun adding row upon row of cedar shingles, working from the bottom up, adorning the existing siding with a fresh wooden skirt.

"You have to consider the edges," the man in the building shop outside Seattle had said when we asked about the difference between shingles and shakes. "Shakes are split, not sawn," he said, loading a bundle into the back of the truck we had borrowed. I ran a finger along the edge. The tiny splinters caught against my skin.

Salt

That summer we talked about having our own place. "Build the whole thing up with our own two hands," Joe said, measuring the exposure on each corner of the wall and then reaching for the chalk line to mark the level row. And I said, "Sure. Somewhere by the ocean," and reached for a sack of nails. One at a time positioning the shingles against the wall, a half-inch seam between them, we secured each piece with two nails. Nearby an air compressor growled and groaned. When our hands tired we switched, our arms tangling as we exchanged nail gun or hammer, nails, the slick saltwater of the skin, wondering how to make it three thousand miles from San Juan Island to New York City before August.

Skin

It is difficult to reconstruct the experience of depression, where the flesh and body of a story fragment into its mere skeletal frame. But there are definitive landmarks, the femur and tibia of memory, which are easier to recall: visiting the doctor, all slow-voiced and gentle, when I was a girl; the fits of laughter blending into an abyss of hysteria; and later anxiety attacks, insomnia, the tiny cuts I made like chisel marks following the lifelines and creases of my skin, the dull purple ring below my palm after I banged my wrist against the wall, the pain washing over me like a drug. Bruising took to my body like a lover—all roughness and whispers. It is difficult to recount the way these things begin, how (gradually and then, yes, all of a sudden) I started noticing objects for their sharpness.

Marble

I have stood for hours before the work of Bernini, fallen in love with the baroque genius who built the city of Rome, smoothing one marble surface at a time. I have studied the bust of Costanza, the lover whose face the sculptor scarred out of rage. And, too, the *Martyrdom of Saint Lawrence*, being burned alive on a gridiron, writhing like an animal. Or the *Ecstasy of Saint Teresa*, pierced by her visions of a heretic, captured in euphoric madness.

Sugar

"Berserk," my father used to say when laughter took hold of me as a girl and my small body appeared as a "jumping bean on a sugar high." Those days my mother watched me closely—the way I binged on sweets and sadness, complained of an itch beneath my skin, grew hysterical with laughter—knowing something of the open pore that I was, and the mercurial border between my extreme seriousness and wild frenzy. Even my brother, inured to my vicious tantrums, my flailing body, learned how to make a cage of his arms as a boy, how to be a good brother, to pin me down so I wouldn't hurt myself, to hold on tight.

Soap

At day's end, Joe and I returned to the woods, to the outdoor shower behind the trailer. Joe traced a bar of soap over my back where the sun had left shadows on my shoulders. He washed my hair, tugging at it gently as I pulled him close. I could sense the play in his touch, somewhat restrained, as he handled me with care. In 1993 Janine Antoni created *Lick and Lather*, a series of fourteen life-size self-portrait busts, seven cast in chocolate and seven cast in soap that she resculpted using the very methods the title promises—her tongue lapping over the forms, her hands washing herself clean—resulting in an array of partially effaced portraits. I wonder how it would feel to hold myself that way, cradling my head in the bend of my arm, taking the pulse and temperature of a body that I want to devour like Godiva or bathe entirely away.

Bark

The deer has no sense of self, yet Artemis deemed all deer sacred, harnessed them to her chariot as she reigned deity of wilderness, childbirth, and virginity, protecting young girls, relieving women of disease. Daphne, loyal follower of Artemis, refused lovers and wished only to be alone. As she ran from Apollo's pursuit, her feet turned to roots, her flesh to bark, hands and hair to the leaves of a laurel tree. I've read that Daphne's leafy fingers were so delicately carved that Bernini's marble swayed in the wind and chimed like crystal. Is art and mythology so different from reality—where simple substance carries divine subtext?

Chalk

Most days we worked through morning. Holding each end, we steadied the chalk line before snapping the center. When the dust cleared, a faint line scarred the wall. We lined up the shingles, alternating large and small to overlap the seams of the previous row. I held them straight. Joe hammered at the nails. Every other row we switched position, the chalk disappearing beneath each layer, like all the drafts for architectural achievements, the burned sketches that informed baroque masterpieces, charcoal marks left on marble before it is cut, lines between insecurity and intent, all gone.

Rust

After a month on the island, we found an ad in one of the local harbor newspapers that read, "1988 Chevy Nova. Brown. Free," and took it as a sign that it was time to move on, head back. And all I could think about was rust and burnt coffee, the metallic taste in my mouth before panic strikes, or the dull bellyache after a chocolate binge.

Chintz

About that time, somewhere in New York my mother was writing poems about fragility and the fear of losing a daughter. Maybe that has something to do with why I stayed away so long. I hadn't seen her in months, since she flew to Colorado, where I was living that year, to be "close by" because I was drinking too much and had grown wary of the kitchen drawers and the sharpness they held. We ate take out and watched old movies with men in overcoats and women with misty eyes. I slept curled in a queen-size bed in her room at the local bed and breakfast, surrounded by stale potpourri, wishing I could blend into the doily surfaces, staring at the uneven seams of wallpaper and trying to will the flowers in line.

Iron

With each row we moved higher up the wall. We were edging closer to the end, which was less about completing a summer job than about the precipice that seemed just out of reach. I felt stripped of my own edges, my siding refurbished into something new, a pattern I couldn't fit in, couldn't breathe in. I thought about how I used to singe my skin with a hot iron when I felt strange and lonely, which was most of the time—a mark on the timeline that I could never bring myself to reveal. Instead, I hid the scars beneath the covers of sex and oversized sweaters. Joe was somewhere by my side asking about where we would stay in New York, if there was work, how we would eventually get back to Colorado, finish college, maybe live for a while in Manitou Springs. We moved higher. The scaffold, little more than a tower of wrought-iron beams and a plane of driftwood, wobbled beneath us. The sun grew hot on my shoulders and simmered my skin . . .

Fire

Hammer. Nail. Hammer. Nail. The dust of cedar and chalk felt like sand in my eye, cutting along the cornea, beneath the lid. But it was my hand I was pinching instead, pinching and then raising. Raising and cocking to yield the interior of thin veins. Cocking and hammering against the wood plank of the scaffolding. I pummeled my wrist against the surface, the bone ignoring the line of skin, which grew pink and raw. I heard Joe shouting. I heard him stumble on the mess of tools, catch and tangle in the chalk line, trying to reach me as my arms hurled toward the wood plank, like hot steel against an anvil—glowing, burning. Joe braced himself behind me and pinned me down (he had learned along the way to do this, too), his voice pleading in my ear.

Gauze

I once overheard a police officer asking a woman if her missing boy had any identifying birthmarks, any scars, and I wondered if he recognized the knife in his own hands, the razor blade that his tongue had become, carving into her skin. After my transgression with the iron—after the burning, that is—I was sent to a therapist whose surname was Dove. He had a Bob Ross way of speaking in a hum, which unhinged me from the start. So I holed up with my silence, fingering the bandage on my arm and thinking of soap commercials and white birds—how we market them as symbols for peace, as if some shackle or cross they must bear—the way once snow gets dirty there is little one can do except wait for it to snow again.

Glass

Twice I saw the doe that summer. When I looked up she stood motionless a few paces from the porch, the fawn grazing by her hind legs. She bent at the neck, craning toward the dry grass at her feet. Her coat was a pearly beige against the white of her tail and spotted haunches, the glass marble of her eyes. Her ears perked and she reset her stance. From a distance I heard Joe's steps rattling the ladder and the angry clamor of a hammer—angry because I had done it again: lost control in that way he could never understand because I would never let him. A day would pass before he would look me in the eyes again. When I turned back, the deer were gone. Or rather, leaving. Had I wanted to catch them, they would have already reached the trees.

Hide

At night, while Joe slept, I slipped into the soft skin of one of his old shirts. Outside, the dry ground was cool against my feet. The air licked at my legs and stirred the hair on my arms and neck. On the island, darkness always made me think of the animals it held. Sometimes I think I could enter the woods and never return, give up everything— all human preoccupation—for the camouflage of hide and instinct.

The damp grass stuck beneath my thighs as I reached over my outstretched legs to grab my toes. And then I felt Joe behind me again, his torso bending along my back, his fingers threading along my ribs, kneading my hips. His breath warmed my ear as he whispered something about a junk car and a free ride.

Fossil

The car was a beater, too. The rusty brown 1988 Chevrolet Nova, listed in the ad we had found, had two missing windows, a cracked windshield, and a broken taillight—and that, just the body of the beast. The engine had logged over 188,000 miles. "At this point it's just clutter in the field," the owner said. As he spoke, the old man, who lived in a cottage by the shore, pointed to the far end of the yard where you could, if you craned your neck a bit, make out the shape of a car beneath the overgrown weeds. Joe started unearthing the vehicle in a skilled excavation, firing off a strand of questions, noting the state of the tires "after all this time." The man smelled like whiskey and chickens, and he kept muttering on about second chances. How "she" could use another stab at the open road.

Dew

I sat on the porch with a cup of coffee, watching Joe clear the car's interior and wash the body. In another minute, the cold spray of water startled me. Wiping my eyes, I heard Joe laugh and I ran to him to wrestle the hose away. For the first of many times we kissed on the hood of the Chevy. Looking up at the garage, Joe said decidedly, "Let's finish this today."

He started on the shingling. I rinsed down the car before joining him. I circled the body of it, which even in its dull matte finish glistened in the morning light, the water beading like dew or the faint mist left on the skin after sex. Years later I would find a photograph of Joe from the end of that same summer, having made it not only to New York, but elsewhere on the east coast. Bare-chested in a pair of khaki shorts, he stood on a wooden dock threading a fishing line. The sky was overcast. His shoulders were wet with lake water or sweat. He bore the same smile laced with hope and anticipation that he often did—a smile that buoyed us, that, for a time, likely kept me alive. On the back side, I had inscribed the words "at Bumpy's house in Maine" and, smaller in the top left corner, "I love this boy." Standing before the Chevy, I wiped sweat from my neck and arms, blotting the skin on my wrist, which was stormy and sore. I leaned my forearm flush against the lip of the car door, the same way Joe and I used to compare skin tones, and noticed the crack in the car's windshield, trailing through the glass from one side to the other, creating a crooked horizon.

Deer

And there, the second sighting: the doe, with fawn in tow, stood upright by the side of the car. Her smooth coat nearly matched the dusty brown of the dented car doors, where soapy spots had begun to dry into a gauzy web. The deer's eyes were dark, forgiving. She stood just for a moment, and then turned and stepped—stepped and then bounded, her hooves pounding softly on ground, pounding and then fading away.

Cells

Nearly at the roof, Joe motioned to where a bare spot marked the crested point of the wall's peak and said, "The last shingle." He scanned a batch of half-size shakes. Weeding through the larger scraps, he felt the face and sides of each piece, as if they held their own cellular composition, like fingerprints or snowflakes, until he found the right one. His eyes were wide and clear as he chalked the wood scrap with the correct angle of the eaves to create a triangle and lined it up to cut. Sitting on the deck of scaffold, with the unearthed Chevy below,

Joe slid the utility knife through the cedar with exact swiftness and perfection before the blade jostled free. Before adhering it with nails, we scrawled our initials on the back of the final shingle, where they would remain, another inscription that may have been my idea—so desperate was I to leave an impression on the world—secure in the unseen grains of cedar at the peak of a structure we hadn't built, but had resurfaced.

Tissue

In order to capture the expression of Saint Lawrence, Bernini reportedly thrust the flesh of his own thigh against fire. Studying his image in a mirror, he chiseled the details of a solitary figure in a visceral emotional state. Beyond the anatomical precision—the twist of the body stretched liked an animal—the life study led to years of scholarly inquiry into the immediacy of human expression, caught between physical agony and a perverse calm bordering on rapture. Perhaps Bernini's gift was an intrinsic understanding of surface. In the same way, Salcedo capitalized on the properties of concrete to create a crack in the floor. When asked how deep the fissure went, Salcedo said, "It's bottomless. As deep as humanity." When I think of that crack, with its rough edges and unknown nature, when I think of Antoni consuming and cleansing her self-portrait busts, I think of the self, how we come to know the materials of the body and the brain: the substance of being alive.

Bone

This is not an endorsement. Nor is it a primer for pain studies. But perhaps a plea for a greater tolerance for rage, and the myriad ways our human impulses are unearthed and revealed: in a rusted tailpipe, in the smell of cedar or soap. Sometimes I still itch beneath my skin, drink too much and sleep too little, grow thin like a stray, think I hear things in the dark, but generally I'm okay. Sometimes I find myself writing the words *doe-eyed* to describe my first love. A particular shade of beige, a certain make and model's tan interior can instill calm and chaos, ecstasy and madness, which makes me think that love must have something to do with bodywork—carburetors and gaskets, bucket seats, and radio knobs. In the junkyard of learning not to hurt myself, I found pliant flesh, the surface of skin, the scaffold of bones, even as the stubborn impulse to damage crept close, sidling up like a deer I knew one summer—or felt I knew, the way she seemed always to be there, tsk-ing at me to stop with all the pain and hurting—before she leapt toward the tree line and receded into the woods.

Lost Wax

Every time I wander through a Greek and Roman sculpture court, a mezzanine of antiquities, I want to be disassembled: to have my arms up to my shoulders fall off as I'm taken from Florence to Pompeii, or maybe end up at the Metropolitan or the Louvre having lost my legs. To be stolen, looted by strangers, and feel the tip of my nose, the cap of my knee, chip and blow away. The phantom pain of dismemberment like the rise and fall of panic and desire, like a drug I once took—a mere dose of it laced with an addictive sadness. I feel this not just in the company of larger-than-life statues of gods and goddesses, the late Hellenistic and half-cloaked heroes, but also before the busts of Minerva and Dionysus, funerary stones, engraved papyrus, terra-cotta kraters, polished capitals and finials, sarcophagus tombs, and headless torsos. These sculptures reveal nearly all of the materials the ancients had on hand: marble, limestone, bronze, and clay. Above all they are artifacts, fragments, the embodiment of classical idealism cast from a mold that no longer exists; only the impression remains.

————————

Years ago, driving south on I-25 from Denver to Albuquerque. When the light shifted through the windshield of the Ford rental, I noticed a set of fingerprints on the dusty dashboard. They reminded me. It was there, on the road, that Joe and I loved each other best. We traveled the mirage of freeway, carving the snake roads of south-central Colorado, where big sky meets horizon and plains shine like honey.

I could see Joe's wide grin and dark eyes, his body—long-limbed and wiry—as if he still filled the passenger seat beside me. His free hand scrawled endearments against the dash, as he leaned into the car stereo to sing a line of the Rascals' "Groovin'" ("You and me end-less-ly"), which made it onto nearly every mixtape and CD we made in those days—his tan hands kneading the flesh of my thigh, like a cat pawing its way to a familiar comfort.

But the passenger seat was empty, except for a dog-eared road atlas, a pack of cigarettes, and a bag of licorice I'd picked up from the trading post in Manitou Springs, and over a year had passed since we drove this route together. Joe was somewhere in Los Angeles. I, having recently graduated, was preparing to move back to New York.

This was the same trip we had taken together every fall when we dodged professors, ignored our friends, and fled campus for Albuquerque: the Sandia Mountains and Old Town adobes; neon lights along Central Avenue's motel row; hash browns and green chili at the Frontier Diner, where booths are wallpapered with busts of John Wayne.

Ahead, the road glittered, an impermeable oil spill in the distance.

———

Here, a *Bronze statuette of Aphrodite of Knidos*. Nearby, *Aphrodite Anadyomene* (rising) in marble, nude, with her weight on one leg as she covers herself with a fold of drapery. Aphrodite is shown undressing before (or is she dressing after?) a bath. It looks as if originally her arms reached forward to shield her sex in a gesture that both concealed and accentuated her form. She carries an air of modesty, but the smooth marble begs to be touched. I imagine its surface cooler than the bronze, more soft, lovelier only in the way that a breast is more welcoming than a shoulder, an inner thigh more inviting than a knee.

———

We met in college, six thousand feet above sea level, at the foot of Pikes Peak. Joe found poetry in hip-hop, freedom in skateboarding. I thought just about everything boiled down to literature and politics. We hailed from opposite coasts but similar bohemian upbringings and, ultimately, split families. I was nine when the once-cluttered walls of our family's Bronx apartment hollowed into silence—into the separate apartments and alternate weekends of my parents' divorce—which may have been the foundry for my restlessness and, in the same gesture, my admiration. My parents were artists, after all—and young. In turn, I carried a certain wariness of inheritance: I wanted the art; I feared the madness.

Each fall, we rode boxcars to Denver and back, hitched rides to the farmlands south of Pueblo or all the way to Albuquerque. Driving the same highway, merging around a jostling truck, I remembered the time nothing but big rigs picked us up, carrying us southbound. Just past the Colorado state border, we were held at a weigh station and questioned by the highway patrol. A toothpick-sucking officer who smelled of hunting season—firewood and jerky and hide—kept scolding, "This isn't the sixties anymore. You ever heard of the bus?" which only strengthened our resolve. Back on the road, Joe cupped my face in his hands, thumbing the crease behind my ears, fingering the slope of my nose, the tautness of skin against cheekbone, like a sculptor claiming the contour of his form.

These were the stories that fueled us, as we collected anecdotes of adventure and philosophizing strangers, *The Dharma Bums* kind of stories, tales of wild hearts surveying open lands for new signs of life.

———————

Here, a plaster model for *Cupid and Psyche*. The mortal Psyche is being rescued in the winged Cupid's embrace after falling into a deadly sleep from which only his kiss would wake her. Cupid has just arrived; his wings rise high. Though it is just a model, you can see the points where the two figures merge, how even in replica, the unblemished plaster reveals the softness of Psyche's mortal hair, the transparency of Cupid's wing, the plush folds of drapery, the fullness of flesh.

———————

I had planned to stay the night in Corrales but decided to stop at some hot springs before crossing into New Mexico. At the first exit past Walsenburg, I drove west toward the San Luis Valley, a stretch of 122 miles bordering the Sangre de Cristo and the San Juan Mountains that harbor the headwaters of the Rio Grande. Along the road billboards boast of cultural eccentricity: the UFO Watchtower in Hooper; the Gator Farm just north of Alamosa, where owners sustain over a dozen Florida alligators with water pumped from the springs. This is perhaps my favorite leg of the lower forty-eight states: vast land of the bizarre and unusual.

How many times did Joe and I swear to stop as we passed the road sign for the Watchtower? How many times did we instead pull off the road near the old candy store and, with a clear view of the tower, snack on licorice and rolled cigarettes while nuzzling over a crossword puzzle or Scratch 'n Win ticket as the car's engine purred? That was how it worked. Ecstasy lay in the splendid distraction of desire.

I may never know for sure, but I've come to suspect that my parents grew fatigued in a sense, that their reality trumped their ideals, that the love itself was left behind like an over-the-hill hitchhiker who forgot to hoist her skirt as the men drove past. But there were other misconducts, infidelities, too, which is why I've grown fearful of borders—fence posts on an open range—between faith and forsakenness, between betrothal and betrayal. These terms are merely words I've come to toy with, their letters circling my mouth like horses and buffalo caught in a corral. And perhaps Joe and I fell victim to the same miscalculation of ideals. As if the thought of stillness would break us, we kept moving, kept knowing each other until the frontiers of each of us became one muddled conquered land.

Here, a *Marble torso of Eros.* You can see the delicately modeled surface, the sinuous curve of the spine. The original bronze resembled a young Apollo holding an arrow and poised to slay a lizard on a tree. But here, Apollo has been transformed into Eros. Look long enough and you might see the remains of wings on his back.

Perhaps Apollo captured in bronze was no less supple than the same figure, now Eros, in marble, but its opaque surface is somehow more pure. And isn't it odd to think that a marble surface comes from a chisel while bronze is cast from a mold? I admire the work of the committed carver. I imagine the act of chasing and sanding as a journey of erasure toward precision. The Greeks, and in turn the Romans, were masters—obsessively so—when it came to capturing the ideal, the kind of perfection now relegated to mythology. So what can be said of us mortals? Why do we so stubbornly aspire to such flawlessness?

At the San Juan National Forest, I pulled into a nearby campground. The access trail to the Rainbow hot springs snaked around shaded forest campsites, waterfalls, and streams and up a canyon rim to reach several inlaid pools. The smell of sulfur blended with the damp scent of spruce and fern.

Throughout the state, thermal wonders spring from small ponds. Early trappers and explorers learned of the springs from the Ute and Cheyenne. Then Kit Carson's scouts herded the local tribes onto reservations, claimed the springs as their own, and built spa resorts. In 1887 the Denver and Rio Grande Western railroad brought the first visitors to Glenwood, where, history buffs claim, Buffalo Bill Cody and Doc Holliday were regulars at the poker table, where Roosevelt and Taft mixed mineral water into their cocktails. Ever since, the pools have offered old-time stimulation to baby boomers, hippies, New Agers, tight-muscled ski bums—to the weak and wobbly, the lost souls and lonely hearts.

Though months had passed since Joe and I had split up, our last year together had been a slow drain, like bathwater through a cracked tub—a crack that widened with every unintelligible sigh, every misplaced word.

Spain: where I fled for a semester to photograph fig trees and learn flamenco. *India*: where he spent months shooting a documentary film on the Tibetan youth in exile. *Guatemala*: where I traveled in the spring and got lost in the highlands of Tikal. *Maine to California*: the route he hitched one summer, channeling Steinbeck. To say nothing of the time we filled together: months in a trailer on the San Juan Islands, road trips pleading with an asthmatic old Chevy to make it from *Seattle* to *New York*. And again, Albuquerque.

"Go" we would say to one other. At those moments our kisses landed awkwardly on the junction between the mouth and cheek, the anatomical crossroad between commitment and solitude, between stillness and embrace. The place where bedsheets, once crumpled and warm beneath us, stayed cool. Where I retreated into myself, my anxieties surfacing as manic outbursts that would eventually destroy us. This, the place we most returned to—what Sexton called the "again and again and again" of anger and love. How many times can we cast the same pain from a single mold before it recedes into yet another landmark, like a statue in a night-fallen sculpture court?

———

After a two-hour hike I reached the first spring. At the far end of the pool, an old couple sat waist-deep and nude under the glass veil of the water's surface. They were both slight of build. Their skin equally pale, simultaneously taut and too thin—stretched like crepe paper. A pile of linen sarongs lay by the pool's edge.

"Room for one more," the man said. The words fell from his mouth, a warm brogue.

I smiled, remembering the "good look" I had for months worn like a Girl Scout badge, or a heart stitched on the chest of a doll my mother made me as a girl. Or for that matter a nicotine patch, which I tried, like a Band-Aid, to pull off without a cringe.

The woman took in the sight of me. She wore a set of silver rings that glinted in the light as she stroked the water with her fingers. She cupped her hands and, bending at the elbows, let the water shower the inside of her forearms. Wide-eyed, the man watched her play.

As I peeled off a thin cardigan, an oversized oxford, I noticed that the elastic thread had begun to unravel along the shoulder strap of my swimsuit. In front of the couple I felt shy, too long, too bony, my skin untouched for months.

"You some kind of an artist?" the man asked, waving a dripping hand toward my cutoffs.

The worn denim of my shorts was speckled and smudged with paint. *Wedgewood Gray. Prussian Blue. Perennial Red.* I scraped at the dry dollops with a fingernail, remembering the summer Joe and I worked odd jobs on the island, where houses were coordinated to blend into the seaside: the gray and blue of the ocean; the rich cranberry bogs; the violet sundew. I could still see the brush doused with paint, could feel being chased into the woods, where we stripped and fell into the grass. He knelt, painting wide strokes—*White Linen* cool and wet along my ribs—and then raised and lowered himself, his chest flattening against mine, the paint smearing between us. We lay side by side, Joe singing that Rascals song or reciting some Tupac lyric in my ear, the eggshell coat drying on our skin, casting the last mold, the final bust and limb of us.

"Isn't it divine?" the woman said, her voice sultry as I stepped into the pool. The water sheathed my legs and hips, rose to my shoulders as I sunk down to a ledge.

"You down from Denver?" the man asked through the scrim of rising steam.

"No—"

"We're up from Joshua Tree," he said. "Been there for the past twenty years or so, isn't that right, Junebug?" He straightened against the rock edge of the pool, slung his arm around the woman's shoulders, and nestled her in close along his ribcage.

"We come here a few times a year," he added. "Cleanses the soul."

"Henry, let her be." The woman combed her fingers through his spongy white beard as he dropped his face to the base of her neck and suckled at the dip of her collarbone, where a small pocket of water had collected. She blushed—or maybe it was me who blushed—as her eyes grew impossibly green against her pastel skin and long gray curls, which frizzed at her temples and brushed the water's surface. The man turned to her. His hair feathered over the liver spots on his head. Beyond his back, the woman splayed her fingers in a wave, the silver rings flashing like beacons in the fog. The couple's skin held the translucence of vellum. Their bodies swayed in a sinewy tangle. The water rippled around them.

I wanted to disappear, evaporate into the steam, but I couldn't bring myself to move. In the pool's oblique surface, my own skin looked thick and woven. In the next moment, the couple sank beneath the water, which, though shallow, flattened over them and regained its luster. I took this as my cue to raise myself up and out of the pool, mindful not to disturb their tryst. Finally small bubbles rose and broke at the surface and the couple emerged. Hand in hand, floating on their backs, they seemed weightless against their own sagging skin, like corpses resurrected.

———————

Here, Cupid. Here, Psyche. Here, too, I'm reminded of a Polaroid of my parents, straight out of art school, arm in arm, walking through an open field, emanating confidence and conviction. Based on the height of my father's Afro, the width of my mother's trousers, I date the photograph: "circa 1978 BC," by which I mean *Before the Collapse* (as opposed to *After Divorce*). Or here, Joe and I at the height of our own empirical reign, that day we lay painted, drying in the grass, still uninhibited, unburdened, belonging to another time.

I'm puzzled by how often we revere and repudiate the examples set before us. The Romans never hesitated to adapt their own forms from existing Greek works—Apollo, god of prophecy, of art and music, became Eros, god of love. Yet somehow I became beholden to the legacy of my parents' marriage, upholding their free-spirited ideals even when I knew those ideals had failed them. Perhaps all Greek tragedy bears the nuance of allegorical wonder. It's easy to lose ourselves in each other, to grow hot-blooded in both our fondness and our fury, until we become altered, amputated, war-torn and weathered, until we become—if I might circle back to my beginning—disassembled.

———

When I finally peeled myself from the sight of the couple floating, I found another pool the size of a basin, and soaked for hours. The water flushed out toxins like memories embedded in my pores, as if my skin had become a sieve of muslin or gossamer or, for that matter, a shroud of gauze.

On the night of what would become one of our last fights, we sat curtained off in a corner of a Colorado emergency room. I never saw the glass shards ricochet across the bedroom, after he threw whatever it was that he threw against the wall (because I had done whatever it was that I had done—again), but I heard the shatter and the peculiar awe in Joe's voice, calling my name, as blood pooled in his palm. As a doctor sutured his near-severed finger, I remembered the evening just before my parents' divorce, when my father slammed his fist against the kitchen table, fracturing the bones in his fingers. He wore a cast for weeks. I had forgotten the image of that plaster glove until I saw Joe's bandaged hand, as if prepped by ancients for burial.

———

Here, a *Marble capital and finial in the form of a sphinx*. The winged sphinx, with a lion's body and a woman's head, is often placed on grave monuments. This one originally crowned the grave of a child. Two spiral scrolls adorn the capital, designed like a lyre and painted in luxurious motifs and Corinthian spools. Perhaps the Greeks were right. Why shouldn't we have such ornament honoring the things we have loved? Why begrudge impermanence if we can preserve impression?

———

I return often to the image of the weathered couple floating at the hot spring. In a way, I believe I've preserved it: all flesh and bones and lucent skin. They are like Rilke's angels of the *Duino Elegies*, like Robert Hass's angels with their alabaster grace. Like the statues I return to, here. I can admit that I was lonely, and at the time I first encountered the couple, I was eager to uncover the divine, a portrait of Elysian contentment—a baptism of enduring tenderness and carnal affection. But who could know for sure? Theirs may well have been a love renewed, having gone, just like for the rest of us, again and again to anger and pain. But I'd rather not sully the image.

What I do know for sure: my parents would never grow old together, their bodies loving each other with age, and I would never know the curve and gnarl of Joe's bones when we grew delicate and creased. I never meant to uphold such expectations. My parents were not liable for creating an impossible paradigm of lasting love (only, I would argue, for envisioning one), nor were we; we were merely adventurers—and young. But is there an idea more curious, more laced with lunacy, than to blindly believe in endlessness, so far before we need to?

———

That afternoon at the hot springs, I retraced the trail through the pine and aspen groves, through dewy fern and skunk cabbage, back to the road where the sun lingered along the western ridge. The highway hummed beneath the wheels of the Ford. I brushed the dashboard clean of its dust and, through the open window, released it there, *somewhere*, amid the vast dazzling San Luis Valley.

———

Here are Cupid and Psyche, Eros and Aphrodite, in all of their mythic glory and orphic joy. And here are smaller statuettes, too, of the goddess Fortuna, of Neptune, Athena, and Lar. I'm beginning to understand, I think, how Rilke learned to render emotion by turning to the sculptures of Rodin—*The Kiss, The Caryatid, L'Éternelle Idole*—how material textures enclose our living impulses. When I say *here*, I mean the museum galleries where I learned to reclaim myself. After years of incessant movement, I turn faithfully to the stone-solid silence of statuary, bow like a courtesan before its classical grace and refuse to feel alone.

Long ago, many of these forms were sculpted in wax before being encased in metal or clay and fired. This was the method used in ancient Greece and Egypt to capture their gods and heroes, the same method used in Africa to mold their figures and deities. This was the method used by Navajo silversmiths to craft belt buckles and brooches and encase turquoise and stone in silver. The heat draws the melted wax from the form and it becomes "lost," drained from the mold, leaving a cavity for the molten bronze, so that the image before us, the smooth limbs and androgynous angles, is a replica of what once was.

Why, when I walk through room after room of Greek and Roman antiquities, do I think of the exquisite and the peculiar, of love? Because these sculptures are allegories preserved. A buxom statue of a woman bears no limbs. A chiseled torso is cracked and headless. Even Aphrodite is missing the arms that once shielded her heroic nudity, and beneath the curve of her hips, beneath her ripe symmetrical ass, it appears as if the flesh of her thigh has been gouged away. These classical forms, created to uphold perfection, have inherited the imperfection of life itself. Maybe I can breathe a little easier now, knowing that the weight of the deities does not sit so squarely on our shoulders—at least not wholly intact.

IV

Caryatid Carrying Her Stone

Origins

I.

What I want more than anything is to find words to do justice to the taste of sweetness: honey, syrup, caramel, fruit, the nectar I tried to collect as a girl from the honeysuckle vines that grew along the chain-link fence bordering the yard of our Bronx apartment.

"It might take a little time," my mother would say, finding me out on the deck again, a mason jar between my legs. I pulled the stamen out of the yellowed blossom to study the bead of nectar resting on the tiny ball. I wanted to collect the juice. I wanted it to drop like rain and fill the jar.

Instead I felt the stamen like a soft thread on the tongue as the flavor filled my mouth. How many lives were altered in the moment between the first time I tasted honeysuckle and swallowed? How much life can fit in the time it takes for the palate to register sweetness? Someone has given birth, teenagers are falling in love, strangers are fornicating in dark alleys, a child is cutting herself, another jumps from a ledge.

Not long ago, a friend called to tell me that the fruit stand on Houston Street is gone, and for a whole day all I could think about was a boy I once loved. We would stop to share a peach after a movie at the Angelika, wrinkle our noses at the prunes, give names to the kumquats, and see who could keep a date on our tongue the longest before biting and swallowing. All the while he told me stories about the fruit trees in Romania, where he was born. Somewhere, a man reaches into his pocket and slips a lemon drop between his grand-daughter's lips, tells her it cures thirst in the desert and keeps the mind sharp. Somewhere else, another traces his wife's lips with ice cubes as she takes her last breath, while the flowers by her bedside pulse. And I imagine that somewhere a jar is filling with every luster she has known.

Can we preserve the sense of taste? If these were canopic jars used during Egyptian rituals, perhaps it would be the tongue I might snip, wrap diligently in gauze, and place inside the jar, so I could look at it through the raised glass berries and the *Ball* name insignia. I'd add it to the specimens of eye, ear, nose, the rough pads of the fingers, and orient them each in a different direction. These specimens should be gathered in a capsule built sometime in the 1980s, when I stepped fully into my skin and began scavenging through the sharp-edged city for its soft corners and sweetness, most of which I found in my mother's garden because "When you have a garden, you have a king-dom," which is something I might have read somewhere on the cover of *House & Home* while standing in line at the grocery store, or on a bumper sticker somewhere in New England, but that nonetheless feels true.

If I had a kingdom, I would trade it for a light-filled house. If I had a house, I would trade it for a cozy apartment. And vice versa, and again—as long as there was a table set for two, and a jar full of honey. I would make dinner and invite Michel de Montaigne, shower him with bonbons and toffee, saccharine bourbon, a demi-glace, and see if he still claims that "we taste nothing pure." And then I might digress into memory, tell him about my first lesson in indulgence: one part ouzo, which I stole from the neighbor's pantry, one part Kahlúa, which my father kept beneath the kitchen sink—all floral anise and vanilla, syrupy coffee and sugarcane—how it made my body shake, made me swear off sweetness for years.

2.

What I want more than anything is to find words to describe the scent of Sundays: wood polish, lemon juice, sunlight. The smell of Murphy's Oil Soap after my mother wiped down the furnishings—crouch-ing along the baseboards, kneeling before the cedar chest with the moth-riddled linens of dead ancestors who dined on scotch and soda, hosted a weekly bridge night, and retired each day with thin mints and a nightcap after the evening news.

By midday the apartment brimmed with sunlight. The rugs were draped and beaten outside. The vacuum cleaner caught its breath before being returned to the hall closet. I lay on the wood floor, feeling the cool flatness against my shoulder blades. If only I could melt into the surface, flatten into a slab of skin and bone and absorb the polish. And while I'm thinking of smells, I'm thinking, too, how they cling to the invisible cells of the body, the way a man might bring a glove or kerchief to his face and carry the scent of it there on the ledge of his mustache. Sundays: the smell of lemon, butterscotch, shoe polish, and resin, the faint whiff of the neighbor's Kent cigarettes seeping through the pores of the parquet floor.

A German surrealist I met years ago in a Spanish village once sent me a matchbox filled with feathers. They were soft and gray. Phoebe? Titmouse? I was in college then, and he was too old to be sending me miniature boxes filled with nuanced charm—without instruction, without warning. I kept the box half open on the windowsill, and when the light rose like an incubator, the pale gray feathers looked oiled. Each day the image would hatch a new vision of spectacular sadness: a full-bodied Swedish cigarette girl from the 1920s who balances her tobacco tray while being groped beneath a table; a white-faced mime who counts his pocket change each evening in an invisible box and comes up short.

What I want more than anything is to soak everything in—the way the wood binges on the amber oil, swells with moisture, and wakes up dry by noon. Sunday. God's day. In our house, the good books were the gospel of Whitman, Dickinson, Clifton, and Lowell. The polished floors made the hallway feel like the aisle of a chapel, the family chest the pew I would kneel before. Between the hours of ten and noon, the musty pages parted to scents of cedar and citrus, oysters and chamomile, a crushed pinot grape, a crisp chardonnay. Something more exotic than home: another borough; another city; port towns in Washington or Oregon; the British Isles; the Portuguese coast—which may have been where I first started to remember, a "grown-up" then, squeezing a lemon wedge over a lunch of fresh bacalhau and vinho verde.

3.

One of those late spring days when the air wouldn't still, I sat on the small deck outside our apartment, trying to place light in a jar. At dusk, my brother and I would escape outside to catch fireflies in the garden. They appeared, one by one, like pinholes in a construction-paper sky.

As we peered into our cupped hands, their wings hid their light like an overcoat. The night air made electrons and neutrons and stars of the flying bugs, just long enough that they might greet each other, mingle for a while like strangers in a bar. And although my mason jar, whose tin lid I had pierced with nails, was ready nearby to make a bulb, somewhere my mother's voice of reason must have warned, "Perhaps not the brightest idea."

Fireflies were a lesson in white and black, the way my hair was once a chapter on gold, my skin a sermon on gray—the combined sum of my black father and white mother—and how nothing can be contained. The fireflies fell defiantly dim when I placed them in a jar, closing their wings like prudent schoolgirls until I let them go. The dark: only richer with the flickering beads of light. The light: nothing without the depth of the night around it.

In the years I worked in an art museum, I would often sit among the statues, brush against their smooth antiquity, and consider how odd it is that we study every detail of their forms except their color. That, the Greeks left up to us—all white marble and obsidian bronze, the spectrum in between open to our imagination. In which case, perhaps Persephone was a black girl. Maybe Athena had the full lips of a Dominican. And the goddesses depicted in fragments of the Great Eleusinian Relief? I always thought they could be Filipino, perhaps even Japanese. It's similar to the way in old black-and-white films, no amount of set light or scenery can tell us what color dress a woman wears, the hue of her hair or the polish on her nails. If we pierce open the world and let all the color bleed through, would it be just as indiscernible? The titmouse or junco might hold steady, as would a crow or a swan, but would a canary still be a canary if captured in black and white?

Sometimes in memory no amount of light—even if all the insects in all the boroughs burned as one bulb—can make the truth clearer. Once, walking in Manhattan with a friend, we found a dead bird on a street near 5th Avenue. I watched my friend pick it up, his bare hands wrapping the small body in a strip of newspaper, and carry it to the nearest trash can, where he nestled it like a mummy in an empty coffee cup and muttered something in Spanish about the ugliness in the world. And maybe because he is Chilean and said the words just so, we ended up in Central Park necking like high schoolers on the bobbing carousel of horses, pretending we were wild and out west, pretending that we could, if we wanted to, make all of the meanness and unexplained loss disappear into the humid urban landfills.

I have read about the power of imagination, how it takes us beyond the sense of sight and may or may not be attributed to kings and saints—Augustine, Francis—with the gift of vision. Perhaps this might explain how I used to imagine myself as an invisible chorus girl in a classic film where, in the gray background, I wouldn't have to show the other black girls how my knees got ashy like theirs, where I could avoid the white girls admiring my tan, their curious fingers drawn to the kinky roots of my hair. I might have just been Saint Clare of Assisi, Joan of Arc, Nefertiti, and if I wanted to sing, I'd be Nina Simone.

4.

What I want is to find words to be a worthy suitor to touch, texture, and the granules of things: fossils, follicles, feathers, sand. My mother's fingernails are secret messages. When she read to me as a girl, I would hold her hand and rub the face of her nails, trying to read the ridges in their surface, which I wanted desperately to decode like Braille or perforated parchment.

Some days I want more than anything to feel those ridges, to touch them with my lips, the way I might have put my mother's fingers in my mouth as an infant—imagining the texture like a soapy washboard or the grooves in the highway when you've veered off course. A texture similar to the snow-covered steps that I fell down as a girl, the ice carving the skin beneath the sweater on my back, the same patch of skin once scarred by the teeth of a Dalmatian—the same dog whose name had something to do with sweetness (Honeybee, or Honeybun?) and whose bite made me fear the spotty nature of things, black, white, timid, wild, a pendulum between extremes.

There are days I remember the creased face of an old-fashioned lollipop that once sliced so deep it left a scar on my tongue, or the million paper cuts I've soothed in my mouth, like the faint line between a lover's belly and the sex, or the trail left by tears. The seams of the body are like the lifelines of a hardwood tree.

That afternoon in Manhattan when we found the dead bird, I wanted to carry it with us, show it some kindness—a stroll through the park, a decent bottle of wine. I wanted to unwrap its dressing of newsprint and lay it on the stone footbridge under the moonlight so it would feel pretty for a night, before I let it blow off the ledge and fall. At least I could have plucked one feather and added it to my matchbox of feathers, pressed it between my fingers as if the pads of my thumb and the imprint of its down might exchange a secret.

We may never bind and shelve the wisdom of snow or the memory of feathers. They are the poets of another time. I may never know what happens to my falling hair when I comb my fingers through it or when a breeze takes it elsewhere. But I might follow this train of thought out back to the old garden, where a line of sunflowers once swayed in the wind.

Now I find strands of my hair lying like thread against the porcelain of the bathroom sink and I think how at every moment pieces of us are falling. My hair gathers in the shower drain and becomes the wet clump of a girl that used to be. My lover clips his fingernails in the bathroom, and I imagine shavings of my mother disappearing into the waste bin beneath the sink. I wish I could run inside and catch them in one of my old glass jars.

5.

And why not consider the sound of flower stalks in the wind? In my mother's garden, the sunflowers leaned like awkward tweens at their first school dance, all hormones and brightness. By summer's end, their stalks grew thick like torch handles. I don't have much to say about sunflowers except perhaps that when they reach a certain height they become immeasurable, the lankiness of their adolescence humbling. Even the breeze around them hums in applause.

Maybe the sound of sunflowers is superfluous, but there is something about their swaying that haunts me. What I want is to describe the sound of whispers and silence: a woman bending in reverence or submission, another in the child's pose of a concubine, or the doomed mortal Clytie, who so loved Helios that she bowed to him daily.

Once in a Tarot reading I drew the card with a scene of two children in a walled garden. When I first saw the image, it wasn't the warmth of the sun that registered in my memory. Instead, the sound of sunflower seeds cracking between my teeth, like the ghosts of Fibonacci, contained sounds of a distant past: my brother and I carrying on after one another, the shriek of bee stings, the slap and swell of mosquito bites. The secrets we learned to keep: sneaking cigarettes and booze, stealing caramels from the corner store (because my craving for sweets made me fearless) while my mother bought milk and a cup of Irish tea. The sounds that kept us quiet: subway cars screeching and moaning on the elevated tracks of Broadway, a car backfiring in the heat of the summer, a stranger in the building next door bowing a brand-new violin. Suzuki remixed against the boom box resting on the bony shoulder of a corner boy outside the pizzeria where a muffled recording of Pavarotti accompanied the owner as he bent to fill pepper shakers on checkered tables.

A block away, I knelt on skinned knees as my hair turned blonde beneath the sunflowers. I plucked their faces bare of seeds before the birds ever had a chance at them. I remember thinking how extracting each seed was like losing a tooth. And sometimes I would ache for them, cringe at the raw vacancy, remembering my own discomfort if my tongue might graze the bare tissue, wounded by loss—is that touch or taste? The lines blend; the senses bend.

Would we recognize the sound of swaying without the visual experience of seeing stalks move? Did van Gogh tongue the petals of his sunflowers in order to learn their true color? Did he press his teeth into their faces to read the pattern of their seeds? The ancients didn't rely on color to chisel the marble torsos of the deities, but they must have known the touch of flesh, and the sight of muscle on bone. I like to think I would know my mother's fingernails were I blind, that I could read them with my lips. I want to think that if I heard the call of a canary, I would think immediately of yellow. But who can be sure?

If truth is curated by memory, and memory administered by the body—all orifice and pulse—then I remember this: my brother and I cracking sunflower seeds between our teeth in the garden, listening for the ice cream truck, while I spit and rubbed clean the dirt on my knees, wondering why I didn't remember being born. Why wouldn't memory allow us that first specimen, that origin story?

———

What I want more than anything is to find the beginning of things, the roots and etymology of the senses, sentient myths, urban legends. What I want is to find the missing girl I have become, the face I once saw plastered on milk cartons in the 1980s that I now recognize in the bathroom mirror. Maybe she's a little taller now, her body fully colored in, and maybe—though only slightly—she has aged.

My skin is no longer so porous, although pollen and sweetness still bring me to my knees. I still appreciate when classical meets cool. I hate substitute sugars and wall-to-wall carpeting. But what does it all mean? Yes, the poets are still the poets and bless them for surviving. And maybe because of them, some days I still wake up craving the taste of honey. I still insist on polishing the floors in my apartment, so I can lie down lazily on Sundays and listen to the church bells downtown, searching for scripture in the ridges that now mark my nails.

There on the hard wood, I'll write my elegy. I want to be the world's first lover, to trace its contours with my tongue, to stay for breakfast wrapped in bedsheets as it prepares coffee. I want it to tease me a little—*Must you taste everything? Must you touch so much? Who will love you if you carry on in these ways?*—and then in a whisper explain that we are not governed by instinct alone. We puzzle and question. We wonder and make meaning. When language fails, the formaldehyde of memory dispels our unraveling.

When the curators of the future find the time capsules of today, mine will be a mason jar. I want the world to nod indulgently as I confess this, to lick my earlobe and inhale the scent of my hair before clipping a curl into a glass jar and tightening the lid, and then to place it somewhere secret and safe—in a field, perhaps, underneath a canary in a haystack full of canaries.

On Puddling

1. I keep thinking about this girl I once knew who died from a fall, and the construction paper we folded and cut in the shape of wings on the evening of her memorial service. We fashioned pipe cleaners into antennae. We glued on glitter and sequins like iridescent powder on the wings of butterflies. We pinned them to a clothesline and raised the thin rope high into the rafters of the college chapel.

2. I am driving on an unpaved road toward the house I rent in the woods, home from errands and a stop at the bar. In the rutted lane ahead, a small cluster of wings appears, milk-white, black, and orange against the pale mud. I slow just before a handful of them flutter from the ground and scatter like rice tossed in the air. I swerve, cursing at the brambles scratching my passenger door, and then stop, engine idling, to watch.

3. In a 1967 interview with the *Paris Review*, Vladimir Nabokov claimed, "It is not improbable that had there been no revolution in Russia, I would have devoted myself entirely to lepidopterology and never *[one who studies butterflies + moths]* written any novels at all." His family's exile led to hunting trips in the Pyrenees, Berlin, Paris, and then on to North America, where his wife, Vera, drove on their epic journeys throughout the continent. Eventually Nabokov landed in the east, where his butterfly collections remain on view at Harvard's Museum of Comparative Zoology—their wings pinned open in crucifixion, their names cataloged by species, by sex.

4. In town I meet a friend for drinks and listen to her inventory of woes, how she misses her college days, and I tell her that I've had it with the butterflies and country roads. But what I really mean is that I

129

am terrified of running them over, terrified of adding to the losses I've collected between then and now. She laughs and orders another round and tells me about puddling—a phenomenon of lepidopteran species in which they collect on the ground, regurgitate into the dirt, and extract liquid nutrients, salts, and amino acids from the soil. Puddling is a supplement to flower nectar, she tells me, which lacks nutrients the butterflies need in order to reproduce. In most species, puddling is restricted to males and increases reproductive success.

significance of "puddling" *

5. I don't remember the first time I made a list as a girl, but the obsessive tendency has been present ever since, which must have something to with my fondness for classification. In the same way the card catalog is a way to navigate the vastness of libraries, or as accession numbers give order to encyclopedic museum collections, we list things to honor them, or because noting things somehow makes them exist.

6. When I say, "a girl I once knew," maybe I never really knew her at all. Maybe I've just filed away certain details, things I remember: her acute laugh, the dark waves of her hair, that she smoked Camel Lights and always left the filters wet, kept journals in high school, loved a good dirty joke and insects. And maybe I never really knew myself then either. Sometimes I can't recall my own name, don't recognize my handwriting when I find a scrap of paper, a sentence written on a bar coaster or a Post-it Note tucked in a book somewhere. *Things I want to do before I die:* Travel to Africa, Alaska, and Berlin. Spend a year in Kyoto. Fold a thousand paper cranes. Learn French. Bear children. Pilot a plane, and parachute out of it.

*lists

7. Nabokov caught his first butterfly as a boy, age seven, in the woods of his family's country home, Vyra. Russia had been at war with Japan. In *Speak, Memory* he describes how he captured a swallowtail in his cap and stored it in a wardrobe only to watch it escape the next morning, dodging through the air with an intensity, he dramatically revealed, he would only find again years later in Colorado. When he found a set of dusty atlases and scientific periodicals, I imagine he might have looked up the creature's name and written it down somewhere—that this was the start of his life list.

8. What I remember most are the petri dishes she stole from the biology lab and kept in her dorm room. Like a curator, she filled them with insect parts: cicada wings, beetle backs, and fly legs—dried appendages like cellophane or tissue-paper jewels. She had worked out a system, her own web of wisdom. Sealing our hand-rolled cigarettes with our tongues and pinching the tail end, we laughed when she told us about Nabokov's cabinet of insect genitalia. We studied the specimens scattered around her dorm room as we experimented with a selection of pills and powders, which we wiped from our fingertips along our gums, hypothesizing the various effects: which would keep us from drying out, which would keep us up the longest with the gentle buzzing in our chests, which might let us fly.

9. Nabokov developed a particular passion for the Polyommatus blues found largely in South America. By sampling the male reproductive organs, he theorized that the Polyommatus icarus originated from ancestors in Southeast Asia, crossed the Bering Strait, and moved down to South America in a series of waves millions of years ago.

10. I don't know when she caught her first butterfly, but at age twenty-two, her last might have been in the Colorado mesa during an expedition for the field class she was taking on Nabokov's butterflies. She must have read about the Polyommatus blues, cracked jokes about courtship and mating behavior while admiring their majesty—that blue a shade she might brush over her eyelids or paint on her toes. At the memorial, a boy in her class with a soft crush in his voice described the sight of her: the wind-sweep of her hair, her laughter [*the girl*] adding whimsy to the field as she hunted, bounding through the tall grass with her net.

11. Puddling is commonly observed post–monsoon season in India. During mud season in New England, too. So I keep my eyes open as I walk along the wooded roads when the light is high and the ruts in the ground swell erect and eager to dry. When I see the clustered wings in the open road, I stop. Some days up to twenty-something butterflies gather at once. When one sees another they must be reassured that the puddle is rich, and that beneath all the sludge lies nourishment.

In the same way, each time I know someone who has died, not fearing death gets a little bit easier. The list has grown, and I am less afraid of the outcome than I am of the act of dying—the pain, the landing, the waiting.

[margin handwritten note: the girl fell out of window to her death b/ painful way to go]

12. On the night of her death, perched on her windowsill overlooking the athletic fields, she peered out too far. I imagine her there, craning her neck to see if the Frisbee that might have flown through the air below was a rare blessed blue. And when she fell four stories to the ground, having landed in the dirt and grass, she lay there as internal injuries began to kill her while the bells of Shove Chapel chimed.

13. Certain moth varieties found in Madagascar are known to puddle in tears. They hover over and probe the closed eyelids of roosting birds. I try to imagine that. Are we so different from the order of Lepidoptera? We classify them with their segmented bodies and jointed limbs, but what about this ability to drink away tears? Can such strange ritual soothe the heart? Can the single breath of a wing lull our obscure faith in chaos and disaster?

14. Nabokov died in 1977 surrounded by his family. Although fever and congestion were likely the cause, I have read that his health was further threatened after he experienced a fall during his last hunting trip to the Pyrenees. In *Speak, Memory* he wrote, "If my first glance of the morning was for the sun, my first thought was for the butterflies it would engender." I imagine his boyhood room filled with specimen boxes, and the way he might have placed his pins artfully through the thorax of his captures and into the corkboard, dabbing them with cotton, spreading open their wings. Or I picture him as an old hatless man in shorts, swinging his net, slipping and landing, taking a last sip from the ground before he went.

15. The morning after the fall, I cried into the armpit of a lover who let me grapple and pull at his skin, held me while I fought, flailing toward the stagnant and familiar pool of grief. Outside, the campus paths were tagged with graffiti—a colorful trail of stenciled wings stained the concrete. I was careful not to step on them, like cracks in a sidewalk I might have fallen through or puddles I dared not disturb.

16. If life were to consist of classified things—real or imagined, actualities or dreams—we might know ourselves by an index of correlatives, things I will try to learn and likely never get right: How to balance my checkbook. Hand-beaten egg whites. Punctuation. The difference between rhythm and rhyme, between lay and lie. The correct way to spell guarantee. Faith in a god. Faith in prayer. Patience. Stillness. Grace.

17. I think often about Nabokov's search for butterflies and the joy they held, how difficult they are to catch, how quickly they fly before you can ever really see them—that is the shame of the living. After the freak falls and car crashes, gunshots and overdoses, it is the things themselves I've grown to hate: the car, the road, the windowsill, bullets and needles and pills, the trees, the ocean, the air.

18. In 2011, after years of doubt, genetic sequencing trials conducted by the Royal Society of London confirmed that Nabokov's hypothesis concerning butterfly evolution was correct, restoring his scientific reputation. I wish it were that simple. I have no proof to validate the details of her fall, or to vindicate the butterflies that never flew that night. I can't help but wonder that if one of them had flapped its wings somewhere across the world at that very moment, perhaps she wouldn't have fallen, the breeze instead rustling the wings on her desk to bring her attention back inside. I've been trying not to blame them. I've been trying not to add them to a list of regrets: our carelessness, our bad behavior, how fast the world rotated in our inebriated spiral.

19. In the chapel we raised the butterflies high into the rafters. For a long time I would fear ledges, and then I would tempt them wherever I could, shuffling my feet to the cliff sides on the summit of Pikes Peak, standing on bridges and rooftops and peering below, trying not to believe that everything that had happened would happen all over again.

20. Soon after her death, I started seeing a new therapist. Through trial and error, a series of treatments, and a strange ritual of tapping lightly on my knees, she talked me through the raw tantrums and quiet moments of my childhood: the journals I kept in kindergarten when our class raised butterflies from larvae, tracking their pupal stages like

the stages of grief, which may well be the stages of living—so much shedding of our past selves necessary to grow, so much morphing and eclosion necessary to live. This is not to say that it's so immeasurably difficult being young, but it feels no less insurmountable than any other age. Again, my theory lacks proof. Perhaps this is no more probable than my notion of the culpable butterflies.

21. Now my lists, scrawled on lined pages, record mundane practicalities, things I don't fear crossing out: Pick up groceries. Fold laundry. Pay bills. Catch up on correspondence. Research odd butterfly behavior. Wash windows. Call home. I strip the lists down to squares, tonguing the edge of a crease for an easy tear, and then fold them up again into origami birds, fortune-tellers, boats. Exacting each fold with my fingernail, I practice their Japanese names: tsuru for crane, sakana for fish, chocho for butterfly. I find them lying around my apartment stuck between books on the shelves, thrown in the kitchen drawer, some pinned above my desk.

22. Here, again, I am pulled over, standing in the dry caked road, watching the butterflies puddle in the dirt. Again, I am kneeling down with them. When we are young and too busy getting high, we don't recognize we are falling. But it is also true that when we are too busy falling, it is hard to recognize anything—the world too cruel and too exquisite to know that we have flown. If only I had a straw I might probe into the ground that somewhere on earth holds the bodies of my friends. If only I might extract from the muck some leftover salt or tear and add it to my list of home remedies, so I can keep on living, keep writing down words and crossing them out.

Laws of Motion

And of every living thing of all flesh,
two of every sort shalt thou bring into the ark,
to keep them alive with thee.

GENESIS 6:19

I. Inertia

In the absence of external forces, a body at rest will remain at rest,
just as a body in motion will remain in motion.

In August, we waited in the dark for the electricity to return, while a hurricane—by then classified as a tropical storm—made landfall throughout nearby towns. Rain curtained the windows as the storm, which had steadily made its way north from the Carolinas, reached inland Vermont. New York was practically shut down, and because Joshua and I still kept ties to our life in the city, journeying back and forth, I imagined the streets of Manhattan streaming like canals, cascading into curbside sewage drains, as Hurricane Irene crafted a thousand perfect waterfalls into the hollow subway tunnels. But the darkness of the woods orchestrated a harrowing symphony as wind and rain drummed against the windows, echoing through the rooms, empty but for unpacked boxes, rollers and paint cans, a list of renovations tacked by the door. We came here in order to leave the city, which had become routine and corrupt in our eyes; we needed a place to start again, to build something, a place we might one day call the beginning of us.

We sat entwined in the dark, two bodies at rest on our small couch adrift in this place that was new and hollow and waiting to be filled. Nearly still, we held each other's wrists, fingers along the inner bend, and compared pulses as we drank from an endless bottle of wine, its cork keeping our place in an old copy of Neruda's *Sonnets*. Outside, the trees rattled against one another like commuters on a crowded train. The winds whined with fury. The rain fell mightily, and all the high mountains receded as if phantoms in the dark.

"Where do you suppose all the birds go during a hurricane?" Joshua asked, the white of his eyes like pinpricks in the dark.

In the morning, the sky cleared to a piercing blue. The woods outside resembled something Andy Goldsworthy might have dreamt: felled birches and elms had caught one another through the night and, come morning, embraced like steeple beams or hands pressed in prayer.

By midday the governor had declared a state of emergency. Radio updates on road closures sounded as a litany of disaster. Helicopters filled the sky—the National Guard dropped food into isolated towns, as local officials hosting FEMA surveyed hundreds of washed-out roads—pavement crumpled as if asphalt weighed little more than construction paper. Cresting rivers had carved islands out of landlocked villages with the ease of a paring knife. Listening to the propellers flap high in the sky, I wondered how it all looked from above. How do they chronicle an infrastructure's wounds: farmlands and storefronts submerged, houses swept entirely away? Everything upturned by the deluge, as if all the fountains of the great deep had burst.

And we, like others, flocked to the flood zones carrying muck boots and shovels, masks and morale, in an all-hands-on-deck recovery effort I hadn't seen in years—ten years—since we cleaned firefighter boots at the Javits Center and delivered bagged lunches to Ground Zero.

"Maybe it's just what we need," a woman said as we stood on the silt bed of Main Street, our rubber soles leaving imprints in the mud. She paced. My feet stuck to the ground. She and her husband had spent a decade renovating their farmhouse in Northfield. When the storm waters flooded its foundation, the house was left unhinged, a structure warped and buckled and waiting to fall. Her neck craned as she said, "It's not just our homes that need rebuilding." A mask hung below her chin. Tears had left small streams in the dust on her face. As she spoke, I wanted to touch those lines, to record the pattern of her loss, the same way I wanted to draw a contour map of the state, to see how water banks and land had blurred.

She chuckled as she turned to me again and explained—"It's the darndest thing, isn't it?—that sometimes things need to come undone before we can put them back together."

Perhaps this is what Isaac Newton meant when he explained inertia as the resistance to change. Wasn't that why we were driven to move? Fearing our own inaction—nothing to push us, nothing to pull—amid the routine hustle of the city?

But it was Aristotle who dominated scientific thinking before Newton. The world accepted Aristotle's ideas because they seemed to support what everyone saw in nature: heavy objects like rocks and trees and buildings want to be at rest on the ground; light objects like smoke and fog want to be in motion in the air; the stars want to remain in the sky. It took years and a few brilliant minds—Newton, Galileo, Copernicus—to overturn Aristotle's less foolproof ideas. How I wish to step into their brains (to say nothing of traveling back in time), to see, for an instant, how they saw the earth and its variables. And where would we be without them? Still accepting the notion that weight alone affects falling objects? Still assuming that the sun and moon and planets moved, but not the earth itself? Once, heliocentric cosmology revealed Aristotle's vulnerability; perhaps now, natural or man-made disasters reveal our own.

II. Acceleration

Should an external force be applied to a body, the acceleration
of that body is directly proportional to the mass of the body and the
force applied (also known formulaically as F=ma).

In September, driving south toward the city, we waited to hear news from Wall Street, where activists—our friends among them—had gathered in Zuccotti Park. Joshua leaned forward to adjust the car radio. The northern stations were late in reporting the story. Instead of the call-and-response inventory of societal ills, income inequality, corporate corruption, and political influence being rallied against by protesters, a local station aired a story on the plight of two migratory shorebirds confirmed dead after being shot down by hunters.

Whimbrels, long-billed shorebirds known for distance flying, stand over one foot tall and can travel up to fifty miles per hour for more than three thousand miles without rest. The birds migrate each year from arctic breeding grounds in Canada to the tropics of Brazil. Scientists in Virginia used satellite transmitters to track a pair of whimbrels for nearly thirty thousand miles. The birds, which had not originally set out to fly together, each attempted to avoid different storm systems. But the force of the storms, like two armed and impassioned hijackers, diverted the birds off course over the West Indian Islands, where shorebird hunting is still legal. The first bird flew through the east side of Hurricane Irene, landed on Montserrat, and spent a week on Antigua. The second bird flew through Hurricane Maria, which had originated as a tropical wave over the central Atlantic and attained hurricane status while approaching Bermuda.

On the morning of September 12, researchers watched the whimbrels disappear from their monitors. When the first bird's signal resurfaced, suddenly grounded, they thought it was an accident, a technical failure. But within minutes the second bird hit ground. One by one they had entered into the squinted view of a rifle-ready young hunter on Guadeloupe. Both shorebirds were shot down from the sky.

Joshua was angered by the story. I was too, but I couldn't help envying the birds their endurance—or is it sheer bravado that impels them into the eye of a storm? If I were a bird in flight for thousands of miles and found no dry ground on which to set foot, I might throw up my wings, as it were, and turn back. Of course, the birds themselves don't think this way. Migration is a force within that they cannot resist.

We were quiet the rest of the way. Joshua stroked his chin as if trying to smooth the knots of his beard, but it had just nearly grown out. Reaching over, I ran my fingers past his angled jaw to the warm pulse in his neck and tried to remember one of Neruda's lines—something about the mouth and the moon and "extinguished constellations"— but I couldn't quite summon the words. All I could think of was how the stars must fragment and burn before they fade into atmosphere. Ahead, through the windshield streaked with rain, I stared down the Merritt Parkway, spanned by historic stone bridges and lined with the dim silhouettes of trees.

As late as the mid-sixteenth century, it was commonly believed that heavy objects fell faster than lighter ones. Aristotle said so, after all. But Galileo's folkloric experiment—dropping a cannonball and a musket ball from the Tower of Pisa—revealed that the more massive object didn't hit the ground first but the objects hit more or less at the same time. Proof that nature, above human authority, was the final judge in matters of falling bodies. If only the whimbrels had shared such a fate, falling not alone but together. And if the birds didn't fall in tandem, I can only hope they fell knowing how far they'd come, believing that we would mourn the loss. Again, birds have no such concerns. Still, had I known that they were out there during the night of the storm, I would have invited them inside with us. There was room enough for two more.

That night in Lower Manhattan, drums echoed as drenched demonstrators cheered in the streets. Some formed a human chain around their encampment, defying law enforcement as police tried to rid the park of protesters. Some raised their arms as if the sky had opened in defiance of order and restraint. And yes, *rain was on the earth!* Each acidic drop sating their limbs, baptizing their skin in the name of hope—not quite the self-disciplined bodies that lined the counters during southern sit-ins, nor the flailing bodies pumped with psychedelics in a spiraling mob at Woodstock, but their drum circles sounded nonetheless. Each day's small triumph added momentum to a movement yet to be classified. Proof, perhaps, that in the presence of force, unseen or otherwise, bodies at rest will accelerate. How long had the impetus been building like a wave or a river swelling?

III. Interaction
If one body exerts a force on another, that body will in turn
exert an equivalent opposing force. Or, for every action there is an
equal and opposite reaction.

In October, the storm came without a name, unlike the mythic torrents of Irene, though equally blameless and humbling (Irene, from the Greek, meaning "peace," after all). A nor'easter is named simply for its directional winds. When the storm arrived, Joshua and I were visiting my mother in New York, and from the cluttered vessel of her Bronx apartment, we watched the unexpected snowfall. The trees held tight to their leaves. Snow weighed heavy on their boughs: solemn, repentant, their limbs pinned down like captives.

Outside, falling branches echoed in an ensemble of splitting timber. "Isn't there something we can do?" I appealed to my mother. She recalled the last time a storm arrived too early for the trees: 1979, when she and my father, at the time living in a seminary apartment outside Boston, ran outside to shake down the branches in an attempt to spare them. Perhaps it was, as she said, "too late for that." But it was unclear to me if she meant it was too late in the evening, or if we were too late to make a difference.

Downtown, I imagined snow blowing through the city streets, collecting as slush piles along the narrowing avenues of the Financial District. How would the demonstrators fare in the snowstorm? How far had they traveled to huddle in twos under tarps until the skies cleared? How many were homesick? How many were falling in love?

Joshua stared out the window. I paced behind him. We were eager to return to Vermont, worried about the damage farther north. I realized then how the woods, which were still new to us, had become ours since the storm. How seeing roads crack and rivers spill through was like coming upon a wounded animal, stunned but still breathing—you cannot walk away.

"Relax," my mother told us. "You are like birds in a cage, the two of you."

In the morning, as we drive north again beneath a sinister blue sky, the radio issues updates: three million people are without power. Town after town along the parkway is deserted, stores sold out of generators, gas stations sold out of gas. All the way to Vermont's southern border, trees litter the roads; some branches hang, each a delicate pendulum swinging. And here, driving beneath the dangling trees and wondering how long before they fall, I think of Aristotle again.

But this time I think of the way Newton became Aristotle's most infamous successor, blessed with the simple happenstance of seeing an apple fall from a tree. Or so I have read. Maybe it wasn't an apple but a leafy twig, or a strip of bark from an ancestor tree. Nonetheless, I like to imagine how it moved him to discover gravitational force and planetary movement, how it inspired his testament to the fundamental laws of motion, inertial movement, acceleration, deceleration, the motion of the moon, the patterns of comets and waves.

And maybe because we are still waiting to learn the effects of the hurricane, just as we are waiting to learn the effects of protests spreading from New York to Oakland, from Paris to Istanbul, or perhaps now it is because we are also mourning the loss of trees, it feels impossible to breathe. If every action elicits an equal and opposite reaction, what will it be? Joshua clears his throat, and I wonder if he feels the same mass lodged in his chest as I do—an iceberg, a bramble, a swelling and defiant mob.

Lord only knows! A sermon sounds through the car radio's static. We are far from the city now, nearing the North.

I turn the dial, feeling the ribbed knob between my fingers, until I find a Canadian station broadcasting music. The woodwind melody sounds like a Paul Winter arrangement—a little bit backcountry, a little bit soul—like the slow cooing of a dove.

My eyes close. Just for a moment. But when I see the shorebirds abruptly falling, I startle awake. The car has accelerated beneath the weight of Joshua's foot. The transmission groans. We are veering off the road, veering toward the guardrail of the interstate: silver and finite and smooth. I grab Joshua's arm and feel his body jerk as mine had. He regains control and pulls onto the shoulder. Shaking his head, he says, "I'm sorry." His voice is weighted, drained. And I say, "It's all right," and open the door to the cool air and set my feet on the ground.

Despite revolutions of light speed and quantum mechanics, Newton's laws have held sound against nearly every discipline. But we are among those in rural and otherwise isolated corners, who know floodwaters to rise, just as I once lived among westerners who knew the fatal breath of canyon fires, among city dwellers who knew towers to fall. We have felt the earth shake, seen evidence of glaciers thawing and mountains eroding. What if mass alone can create movement, or sheer will can propel us forward? Couldn't the laws of motion just as easily read as sermons against inaction, against inert generations? We cite science and channel scripture for a sense of equanimity amid the chaos. But sonnets reveal as much about sustainability as any lesson on evolution. The human heart keeps its own record of the wreckage.

I never saw the whimbrels that were shot down over Guadeloupe, but somehow those two birds have become my lasting image of the storm. The same way years ago so many recorded the image of two strangers leaping from the South Tower, hand in hand. And perhaps some will remember the young lovers who converted to Islam and knelt to wed amid the crowd in Zuccotti Park. We venture far and return home in order to learn; we topple and rebuild in order to live, sometimes en masse, sometimes in solitude, sometimes in pairs.

Along the barren shoulder of highway, we bend and stretch our legs. I watch Joshua breathe deeply, inhaling as I do, and though I cannot hear his breath, cannot feel his pulse, the rise and fall of his chest mirrors mine. In the sky, I catch sight of a hawk soaring above the trees. I take the keys, and I take the wheel, and we continue on.

Practicing

Walking in the woods, I am trying to find a word for the sound of snow beneath my feet. It sounds nearly the same as always: a methodical crush, with the levity and chance of rolled dice landing with each step—but icier this time, more laden with winter's end. The sun, just peeking over the eastern ridge, gleams along the ground's fresh crystalline layer. Soon, the light will bathe the birches and cast itself longingly against the neighbor's red barn, as if tossing a veil, as simple and secure as an afterthought. I want to think about all of the love stories in history. Instead, I am preoccupied with sights and sounds, trying to authenticate time and place, all our past discoveries and collective human failings.

Not long after moving to the country, I scrape together all that I am worth and buy a house. The house is old and charming and has too many rooms that need to be sanded, painted, brought back to life. The house once belonged to a family that is no longer a family; it has shifted and slanted, seen divorce and flooding, generations of life and death. With the soul of a farmhouse and the upgrades of a Cape, it has a sturdy frame. The property sits between a road and a river, between industry and sanctuary, which is a place I can bear. There is a room with eaves and windows facing both directions that once belonged to a girl. I decide to start there. I collect paint swatches at the hardware store and try to imagine the space anew. *Stormy Monday, Ivory Tusk, Winter Gates.*

Growing up in the city, I used to play the violin. Looking back, I still wonder if, had I learned to play the guitar instead, I might be closer to my father now. His six-string classical guitar was among his first loves. Just like my father, who, as a boy living dirt poor in rural

Pennsylvania, was given his first instrument, I got my very own violin from a family friend. More than one hundred years old, its hollow body was made of rosewood, stained and perfectly aged. The violin soon became instrumental in my understanding of self. When I played, my heart rising to the top floor of my chest, I never knew if I was really happy or really sad. Years later, I felt a similar longing when I first read Frank O'Hara. Or when, in the dead of winter as the snow in Manhattan grew soiled and gray, I learned that O'Hara played piano and sold postcards at an art museum—which was my first job when I returned to the city after college.

————

I am here, but I am always a world away. Months ago I grew obsessed with a story in the newspaper about a Stradivarius that was stolen in Milwaukee. Known as the Lipinski, and over three hundred years old, the violin was on loan to a local concertmaster. Shortly after the Milwaukee Symphony Orchestra's performance of the final sequence of Messiaen's "Quartet for the End of Time" had silenced the audience and ended the concert, the maestro was followed to his car, shot with a Taser, and robbed of the rare instrument. What most compels me about the story is the profile of the alleged perpetrator. A slim-framed black man in his forties who, though he fancied himself a high-end art thief, was a low-level street dealer, a twice-convicted felon fighting to make ends meet and provide for his five kids.

————

I took violin lessons with a woman named Sally, and I always said, "I'm sorry," even when the occasion didn't call for it: if my bow needed rosin; if my E string screeched too high or my elbow dropped low, or because I never felt ready to begin. I remember walking home from my weekly lesson in winter, how the blackness of my violin case looked against the snow, and how when nearing home it grew heavy and knocked against my knees. I remember a lot of things in black and white, but I learned early on that nothing really is. So much depends on color these days. So much always has.

————

The paint chips are splayed on the kitchen table like a deck of cards. I tape them to the bathroom mirror and the humming refrigerator door. *Mesa Verde Tan. Galveston Gray.* I want a rich cream-ochre, something that feels warm and rooted in place. *Kansas Grain. Durango*

Dust. *Richmond Bisque*. With the blank page of winter outside, I can see America taking shape and imagine how I could paint every state into these walls, place an entire nation in a room: *Pewter Dust* for the painter I fell for in the Carolinas, who quoted Ram Dass and placed dull powder between my eyes; *Barren Plain* for the woman in Seville who burned sage for my soul and then told me her plans to move to New Jersey; *Mannequin Cream* for mall windows left shattered in Houston, Newark, Baltimore; *Cloud Cover* for a thief in Wisconsin plotting a heist as he, a rare black man in the concert hall, attends the symphony.

———

When I was seven or eight I played my first recital, hosted by the family of another violin student who lived in a house across the parkway (our version of "the tracks"). The oversized Victorian sitting room made me feel like a prop in a movie set, or a doll in a dollhouse—everything from the grand piano to the paneled walls was pasty and pastel, like most of the girls who played that day. All short skirts and bony legs, we took our places with our sheet music and rosined bows, as a large swatch of sun came through the bay windows. My father, with his black turtleneck and neatly trimmed Afro, sat somewhere among the chintz-covered dining chairs next to my mother, her bare feet in Birkenstocks, who was noting the light before it crossed the Hudson and settled over the Palisades. That afternoon, glancing at our bows moving in sync, listening to our strings piercing through Suzuki variations, with only the occasional squeak out of tune, I realized that I can move inconspicuously between worlds: black and white, urban and rural, between privilege and lack thereof. I would spend many of the next formative years feeling out of place yet managing to belong. Passing with little impact on the ground beneath me, like an animal in the woods at night where the snow covers all tracks by morning. As much as I love the country, I fear love for the way it blankets everything it knows. Perhaps that is why I may never stay.

———

In the city I can lean out the window of my mother's apartment and peer down over Manhattan: passing the South Bronx, I am the elderly woman watching the block; in Spanish Harlem, my arms are the twig arms of a boy manning the fire escapes of the barrio; on the East Side I am the park and its darkness that a million trees try to breathe away;

on Broadway, I am a stagehand; in Times Square, I am the neon coil in a lighted sign; in Chelsea, my arms bulge and tighten, my hips slant; in the village, too. I am Stonewalled. I am waiting for the Supreme Court to strike again the way it did for Loving in Virginia, the way it did for my parents. And it won't be long until *Obergefell v. Hodges*, until dignity in the eyes of the law "is so ordered" once again. I am stoned in Alphabet City; in the deep bowels of the Bowery, I am both artist and trick, perusing the changing sky before kneeling and crawling through the back door of the Chinese Arcade; I am Italian bakeries, Ukrainian church pews; at the Seaport, I am the anchorman hung over the bow; and then I'm crawling again onto the ferry docked on the island where so many began, where so many licked the shores of America, to write their own names for the first time. To have a name.

———

After days of uncertainty, staring at a spectrum of shades, I settle on *Montgomery White*, which feels fitting and elicits a warm familiar friction: Parks and King, boycotts and marches, lilies and handmade paper and fresh-fallen snow. For nights I have a dream in which I am wearing pajamas and crawling through a battlefield of cowry shells searching for black marbles. In the dream I can hear the crush of shells, as recognizable as that of snow beneath me. My knees are cut and bruised and someone is cupping them gently in his hands. There is a boy nearby holding a stone behind his back. When I wake I realize it is not a boy but my father—or rather, a drawing he made in the early 1970s of a boy staring up at a mounted police officer on a gigantic white horse. The next week, I travel back home to the city and spend an afternoon strolling through the discreet wing of musical instruments at the Metropolitan. I listen for the silent resonance within the wall cases.

———

In the newspaper I look for more news of the Stradivarius. Instead, I find an article in an online edition of *Vanity Fair*. The rare violin, one of only several hundred made by seventeenth-century master luthier Antonio Stradivari said to survive, is of "unquestioned provenance," its worth in the range of $6 million. Yet no one seems to know exactly what makes Stradivarius violins so uniquely famed. The varnish? Indigenous wood from Cremona? Perhaps what led Stradivari to his genius was a sheer intuition for the nuances of acoustics and the minute alterations of body and space. The Stradivarius demands action. Its basic need for equal parts admiration and attention makes it all the more compelling: it must be played, handled, moved. Perhaps it is as restless as I am, filtering between the pristine grace of country-side and the necessary wear of the city. Maybe Stradivari understood this. If he was in fact a genius, he might have also been, as Aristotle would have us believe, a master of metaphor, able to perceive likeness in dissimilarity, the gray area inherent in matters of black and white. Ultimately, the stolen violin was recovered, intact and unharmed, by the Milwaukee Police Department. In every report, authorities take care to outline the various methods of confirming the authenticity of the rare violin. But how can we ever know for sure?

———

Here in the snow, a rabbit's track. Here, the print of a deer. Is this really the deer, or has the rabbit become a master of disguise, bound-ing in zigzags on heart-shaped leaves? I want to shout out descrip-tions, look up their scientific names, give words to their shapes, clas-sify their existence—but I already know these tracks. I learned them as a girl. Not only do they have names, but, by now, I think they hold their own notes. The three-pronged relief strums rabbit. The rounded heart chimes deer. If only I could remember the fingerhold for each sound—call all these creatures out from the tree line. Instead, I finger the strings of my scarf; I pluck at the toggles on my coat. I am still try-ing to find my pitch, trying to master cadence: one rhythm belonging to the city and the other to the remote woods. In the no-man's-land in between, I am a petty thief, a master of the heist. I am a refined concertmaster, a common fiddle needing to be played.

———

By the time I reached high school, I played my violin when I was lonely, which seems so obvious now. Tacking sheet music to my wall, I practiced with persistence—a canon, Bach's concertos, Mendelssohn. Reading notes came with ease—euphoria, even—as a language I understood and guarded like a secret crush, a rebellious obsession. If I left my bedroom window open, the sound echoed against the neighboring building, the same structure that caught and reflected the afternoon light. Often I repeated the same piece three or four times, as if rereading, as if seeing something new. My arm flowed back and forth, wrist loose, the bow weightless between my fingers. The closest

I have come to such weightlessness was when I first saw Greek and Roman statues as a girl. The museum, the one place I can stare without feeling bashful, where, during a middle-school field trip I first felt aroused by the smooth perfection of form imperfectly preserved. And then again, years later, I would fall in love in those same galleries with a sweet-talking museum security guard, a painter, whom I would eventually take home, introduce to my mother, share a bed with—the one with whom I left the city and moved to the country and bought an old house. He knows I am mourning my violin days when I remind him, again, "You do know I used to play, don't you?" and he nods, although I'm already at him with, "Or have you forgotten?" He humors my longing without missing a beat and puts on a record, something soulful like Etta James or Nina Simone. He knows that I cannot be satisfied with only one view, that my happiness is laced with unease, a chameleon longing. I am thankful for that. I'm thankful, too, that I can retreat to the country and the city, to live in the extremes of anonymity and silence. There, I cannot be evicted, can no longer be stunned by loss. There, I will paint the walls gray and practice being alive.

———

Before the paint there is the primer, and before the primer, there is the need to prep the walls. In the room that would become a small study I find generations of wallpaper, which I peel only to unveil new layers. The underside of the paper is the color of certain eggshells, a parcel, coffee with cream; it spans the spectrum of flesh. Like a snake-skin, like a sunburn, it peels in stripes and patches. The sheds blanket the floor. After hours of this I stand amid strewn strips wet with glue. The room looks as if a protest or a ticker-tape parade had taken place and left only a damp scattering of pamphlets and fliers—no trace of fleur-de-lis or blue-willow-patterned wallpaper—calling for a revision of history. The walls will be sanded smooth and painted gray and lined with simple shelves for books, which is the only thing we really own, so I can find O'Hara whenever I need to, so I can reference the language of others and grow strong again.

———

When I was young I thought that everything was just practice, a rehearsal for life, which at some point would simply begin. Some days I still want to believe this. There is no rehearsal for living, of course, but sometimes it does take practice: loving the fact that you were born, loving all the winters, the inevitable seduction of *elsewhere* or *other* that builds like a scale or refrain and can trail on and on like a sentence.

————

In just weeks the ground will thaw. The last licks of snow caught in the shaded wood will carry a new pitch beneath my steps: deep, wet—the coarse slush like rosin against an open string. And my boots will sink deeper into the muck of the coming mud season. But here, now—this is what it means to linger, before the call for "Last frost" when we all order big, steal a final glance, before any signs of warming. This recital is not nearly the last. No matter where you are, city or country, the sound of snow crunching underfoot is pretty much the same. But I still can't figure out how to describe it.

Immortal Wound

Actias luna (Linnaeus, 1758)

MONTPELIER, VERMONT

To think I almost missed it—the small incongruity that lay on the sidewalk beneath the lamplight of Main Street. Though difficult to see, when I crouched down, the form of a luna moth at first appeared in its stunning wholeness as if it might merely be at rest. But when it didn't rouse as I approached, nor budge when I drew a finger to its wing, I knew the moth was dead.

Nearby, lovers stumbled from the bar, clutching one another through the back pockets of their jeans. As their whispers receded down the street, I knelt, pinching carefully, and placed the moth in my hand. Yellow margins accentuated the hind wings' curving tails. Purple lined the top of the forewings—a pale purple, like drowned lips or hypothermic skin. At four and a half inches, its pale green tissue-paper wings filled my palm, which grew clammy, a little smitten, in the summer night—and, indeed, it *was* summer again, and the air was swollen and my skin was lonely and I was wishing New England had fewer churches and more sky.

When I felt a sudden stir, I thought there might still be life in the moth, that she was not in fact dead, but dying. But it was just the wind stiffening her wings. I feared then, with the moth's lightness, that the same wind might take those wings, that I might lose her. The late-night chill made it hard to tell if the warmth in the cradle of my hand sprang from the moth's underbelly or my own budding grief.

Just then, I envied Woolf her day moth zigzagging against a window-pane; I envied Dillard the candlelight that singed her moth's wings, its body burning like cinder through the night. I envied these women, each witness to the moment of their moth's expiration, each in her expressive brevity embalming those dying wings.

The death of a moth is a common occurrence—consequence of destined wanderings and genetic attraction. Still, what cruel mystery is a luna, royal silk moth of the deciduous forest, found dead outside a small-town bar? And what justice could I offer but to notice the thin scratch just below the eye of her left wing, like a run in a stocking scarring the otherwise smooth, unblemished surface?

In the pool of night, the moth grew translucent, more blue-green than yellow-green, pearly under the moon. Six legs curled beneath the cotton-like abdomen; two feathery antennae vibrated in the air. We are entering rigor mortis, I thought. But again, it was the breeze cutting between us—between her drying form and my pulsing palm. Her wingtips bobbed in the air to form the letter V. I wanted to whisper into the shape of those wings—*I feel certain that I am going mad again*, or *You have given me the greatest possible happiness*—and then close them gently like a vintage coin purse I once inherited. But I wouldn't trouble her with such things. Too many other questions surfaced as I studied her form: Had she died young? Did she mate and deposit her bounty of eggs? What led her here, now? The flickering glow of the drive-through ATM, the two-screen theater's starlit marquee, the neon draft signs in the windows of the dimly lit bar? Had she tried this once before? How long did she lie there before being found?

What most lingers is the silence I associate with the moth's death—or, rather, her afterdeath. I can't attest to her body jerking in spasm like *a flame-faced virgin*. I can't say she exhibited a *superb last protest* as if overpowered by a mean antagonist. I do imagine her body falling (because I have a thing about falling bodies), her wings flapping like pages of a book and then waving until they looked like wings again. Instead, for me she simply appeared, as if discarded, misplaced, dropped like a folded dollar bill that might have been tucked somewhere and then slipped away like a clue—a lead in a case gone cold—leaving mystery the sole widow of death.

Perhaps we are all insects of longing and luminous dreams: dusky sallow, common house moth, *Actias luna*—strong fliers seeking to mate at midnight, feeding on birch leaves, spinning silk into papery cocoons. Haven't we all fed on the strange beauty of our findings, spun such strangeness into stories, secrets, silence, to insulate and cosset the great uncertainties that leave us stripped, bare? Don't we live to glide along invisible currents, swearing we will find, somewhere on earth, some familiar beacon that knows us? Insisting on nocturnal promise, we are drawn to the spotlights that blind us just as surely as a glaring headlight might steer us off-course or the taillight of a lover driving steadily away can forever burn.

Ever since that night, that moth, that familiar bruised purple, that summer blue, I've been thinking about instinct and ardor. The way they lure and misguide us as eagerly as life and death collide. Wedded like Vegas lovers to the conniving bulb of light, to the forgiving kerosene of the heart, we go down dancing, or blazing, or in a moment unobserved, as if it never came to pass, as if it never even happened at all.

ACKNOWLEDGMENTS

Much gratitude is given to the editors of the following publications in which these essays first appeared, often in slightly different forms:

"On Touching Ground" in *Bellingham Review*

"Honey" in *Sonora Review*

"The Dollhouse" originally appeared as "The Granville" in *Ducts* and was reprinted in *The Man Who Ate His Book: The Best of Ducts, II* (Fall 2013)

"Mirror, Mirror" in *Drunken Boat*

"Still Life with Chair" in *The Normal School*, reprinted by permission of *The Normal School*, copyright 2015 by Jericho Parms

"Of Things Lost" in *South Loop Review*

"A Chapter on Red" in *Hotel Amerika* and excerpted as "Red" in *Brief Encounters: A Collection of Contemporary Nonfiction*, edited by Judith Kitchen and Dinah Lenney

"Lost Wax" in *American Literary Review*

"Origins" in Fourth Genre 17, no. 2 (2015):53–60

Thanks to John Griswold for recognizing something here and shepherding it through. And to all of the wonderful folks at the University of Georgia Press for the work of publishing this book.

The writing of these essays was generously supported by the time and space afforded by the Vermont Studio Center as well as an artist grant from the Vermont Arts Council and National Endowment for the Arts, for which I remain grateful.

I am indebted to the rich and nurturing community of writers at Vermont College of Fine Arts. Thanks to the support of Louise Crowley and Ellen Lesser, and to my advisors Rigoberto González, Patrick Madden, Sasha Feinstein, and Philip Graham, who not only guided me through the early stages of these essays, but have been unwavering in their confidence and support. Thanks to the insight, encouragement, and generosity of other remarkable writers who have helped make this book a reality: Steven Church, Dinty Moore, and Audrey Petty. And for their shared passion and unending willingness to read: Emily Arnason Casey, John Proctor, and Laurie Easter.

Thanks to Rachel Gerstein and Anna Child for keeping me grounded, despite the distance. Special thanks to Joe "Guisepi" Spadafora for trusting me with the portions of this story we shared.

In loving memory of family and friends no longer here who have in some way shaped these pages, in particular to Judith Kitchen, who believed in this book before I did, and whose generosity and spirit made all the difference.

Thanks, always, to Joshua Sevits, for the unending love, enduring patience, and critical eye.

Above all, I thank the members of my family, who have left their indelible impression on these essays, and without whom this book would not exist, in particular my mother, Louise Parms, to whom this book is dedicated ("to the moon and back") with love.

NOTES AND SOURCES

The book's epigraph is from Matthew Zapruder's poem "Global Warming" from *Come On All You Ghosts* (Port Townsend, Wash.: Copper Canyon Press, 2010).

On Touching Ground
Special thanks to the department of European Sculpture and Decorative Arts at the Metropolitan Museum of Art, whose galleries house Degas's *Horse Trotting, Feet Not Touching Ground, The Little Fourteen-Year-Old Dancer*, and other artworks described.

Jesse McKinley, "Horse Advocates Pull for Underdog in Roundup," *New York Times*, Sept. 5, 2010.

Honey
"The day is coming when a single carrot, freshly observed, will set off a revolution" is from *Joachim Gasquet's Cezanne: A Memoir with Conversations* (London: Thames and Hudson, 1991).

Frank O'Hara, "Why I Am Not a Painter," from *Selected Poems*, ed. Mark Ford (New York: Alfred A. Knopf, 2011).

The B Side
The epigraph is from Bob Kaufman's poem "I Want to Ask a Terrifying Question," from *The Ancient Rain, Poems 1956–1978* (New York: New Directions, 1981).

West Side Story, 1961, was directed by Jerome Robbins and Robert Wise.

Quoted material is from F. Scott Fitzgerald's "Echoes of the Jazz Age" in *The Crack-Up* (New York: New Directions, 1945).

The Dollhouse
Thomas Morgan, "New York City Bulldozes Squatters' Shantytowns," *New York Times*, Oct. 16, 1991.

It's a Wonderful Life, 1946, was directed by Frank Capra.

Mirror, Mirror

". . . a girl who played in sprinklers while loving Heraclitus" is from Jenny Boully's *The Body: An Essay* (Athens, Ohio: Essay Press, 2007).

Still Life with Chair

Epigraph and quoted material is from Theodore Roethke's "The Chair" from *The Collected Poems of Theodore Roethke* (New York: Anchor Books, 1974).

Italicized lines are from Pablo Neruda's "Ode to a Chair" in *Odes to Common Things* (Boston: Little, Brown, 1994).

Babel, Notes on Tourism

Epigraph: from Hart Crane's "General Aims and Theories" in *Hart Crane: The Complete Poems and Selected Letters* (Library of America, 2006).

Of Things Lost

"My mother is a fish" is from William Faulkner's *As I Lay Dying* (New York: Vintage Books, 1985).

To Capture the Castle

Italicized lines are from plaques located at the three stations of prayer along the Croagh Patrick pilgrimage trail. Thanks to the Coagh Patrick Visitor Centre, Teach na Miasa, for additional source material.

A Chapter on Red

The epigraph is from Hans Hofmann, as found in Edith Anderson Feisner and Ron Reed's *Color Studies* (New York: Fairchild Books, 2014).

Henri Matisse, *The Red Studio*, Issy-les-Moulineaux, Oil on canvas, 1911

Quoted material (Matisse) is from wall text, Henri Matisse, *The Red Studio* Museum of Modern Art, New York, N.Y.

Quoted material (Rothko) is from wall text, Mark Rothko, *No. 21.* Metropolitan Museum of Art, New York, N.Y.

On Grazing

Maria Newman, "9 Farm Pets Found Mutilated On School Campus in Bronx." *New York Times* (New York, N.Y.), Jul. 25, 1992.

A Theory of Substance

Doris Salcedo, *Shibboleth*, 2007.

Quoted material (Salcedo) is from Jon Henley, "Cracked!" *The Guardian.* October 10, 2007.

Special thanks to the Galleria Borghese in Rome whose galleries house several works by Gian Lorenzo Bernini, including *Daphne and Apollo* referenced and described.

Janine Antoni, *Lick and Lather*, 1993–1994.

Lost Wax

Special thanks to the department of Greek and Roman Art at the Metropolitan Museum of Art, whose galleries house all major artworks referenced and described.

Quoted material is from Anne Sexton's "Again and Again and Again" in *Love Poems* (New York: Houghton Mifflin Company, 1969).

Origins

Michel de Montaigne, "Of Smells" and "We Taste Nothing Pure" in *The Complete Essays of Montaigne*, ed. Donald M. Frame (Stanford, Ca: Stanford University Press, 1976).

On Puddling

Quoted material is from Vladimir Nabokov's *Speak, Memory* (New York: Vintage International, 1967).

Vladimir Nabokov, interview by Herbert Gold "The Art of Fiction No. 40," *The Paris Review*, Summer–Fall 1967.

Laws of Motion

Epigraph: from "Genesis" in *The Holy Bible*. King James Version (New York: Penguin, 1974).

Quoted material is from Pablo Neruda's "Sonnet XVI" from *100 Love Sonnets = Cien sonetos de amor* (Austin: University of Texas Press, 1986).

"Birds Survived Storms Only to Be Shot Down by Hunters" *Here & Now*. WBUR, October 17, 2011.

Practicing

Buzz Bissinger, "The Stradivarius Affair" *Vanity Fair*, October 31, 2014. http://www.vanityfair.com/style/2014/11/stradivarius-violin-crime-milwaukee

Immortal Wound

Italicized lines are from Virginia Woolf's letter to her husband before her death, from *Letters of Virginia Woolf, 1936–1941* (New York: Harcourt, 1980).

Virginia Woolf, "The Death of the Moth" in *The Death of the Moth and Other Essays* (London: Harcourt Brace & Company, 1942).

Annie Dillard, *Holy the Firm* (New York: Harper & Row Publishers, 1977).

CRUX, THE GEORGIA SERIES IN LITERARY NONFICTION